THOUGHT-PROVOKING THOUGHTS ABOUT LIVING . . .

**A collection of epigrams for living,
plus observations about people and life
around the world**

by

DEREK PARTRIDGE

Enjoy!

Derek

This book is obtainable from
Kendall/Hunt Publishing Company
4050 Westmark Drive
Dubuque, Iowa 52002
1-800-228-0810
FAX 1-800-772-9165

This edition has been printed directly from camera ready copy.

ISBN 0-8403-9456-X

Library of Congress Catalog Card Number: 94-76406

Printed in the United States of America
10   9   8   7   6   5   4   3   2   1

THOUGHT-PROVOKING THOUGHTS

For JO & EV

"I have faith in my star – that is, that I am intended to do something in this world. If I am mistaken, what does it matter?"

Winston Churchill (aged 22)

"There is only one success . . . to be able to spend your life in your own way."

Christopher Morley

CONTENTS

PREFACE

This book is designed so readers can browse through it, as each epigram is complete in itself. However there is also a deliberate sequence to the paragraphs and chapters, specifically intended to create a greater understanding of what follows, as the contents are both thought-provoking and controversial

The following biographical sketch of the author's unusually wide-ranging experience of life will enable the reader to better understand his purpose in writing as he has and his credentials for doing so. It was originally written for the 20th Century Fox movie "Savage Harvest", in which he starred with Tom Skerritt and Michelle Phillips . . . working with 40 lions (one of which at him in the film!) on location in Kenya and Brazil.

Derek Partridge describes himself primarily as 'a communicator, who specializes in diversity'. Here's what lies behind that seemingly somewhat flippant statement. He is a writer, journalist, TV talk show host, news anchor, interviewer, corporate spokesman, game show quiz master, radio newscaster and DJ, actor, lecturer and business owner. He is fluent in French and Italian, also speaking and writing German and Spanish.

He was also a professional photographer, PR consultant, European tourist courier and, after winning the Certificate of Merit as the Best All Round Recruit, he became a radar officer in the R.A.F. He was a police officer in the City of London Special Constabulary and trained S.W.A.T. Teams in Rhodesia. He is an international trap shooter and former world record holder.

Born in England, his mother was an American artist and his father, Major Frederick Partridge, O.B.E., was a Police Commissioner who later worked in M16, Great Britain's equivalent of the C.I.A.

Derek has lived in 8 countries and traveled in some 75. He was educated at Charterhouse, one of England's top five Public (private!) Schools and then attended courses at the Universities of Paris and Barcelona.

Derek's lifelong ambition was to become a TV host and presenter. After 20 years of frustrating rejections, this was fulfilled when Mike Hart-Jones* asked him to join Rhodesian TV in 1976. Derek became a celebrity in Rhodesia, where he was the chief TV news anchor and host of "Frankly Partridge", a live magazine show which became the most popular program in Rhodesia. He was also quizmaster for TV's "Kwhizz Kids", hosted several "Message to the Nation" specials and worked as a radio newscaster and DJ for the RBC.

His pamphlet "Rhodesia - as it really is" was described by London's prestigious The Daily Telegraph as: "a drop of truth in an ocean of lies"; over 10 million copies were distributed in 42 countries. Leaving Rhodesia in 1979, when it became Zimbabwe, Derek joined WKAT/ABC in Miami, as a news anchor and host of two daily talk shows. For three years his column "Derek Partridge reporting from America" appeared in Look & Listen, Rhodesia's TV Guide.

Derek's journalistic work began in London in 1961, as a columnist and feature writer for the Daily Express Group's "Investors' Guide". He subsequently had articles published in, eg: The Washington Post, Accuracy In Media, Beverly Hills People, Screen Actor and Drama-Logue. He edited the International Television Director, listing the world's TV Networks.

In 1981 he joined Financial News Network (now CNBC) as a news anchor/writer and interviewer, working on 14 consecutive half-hour, daily newscasts. He hosted "Financial Inquiry", "Hilton Video magazine" and two Specials for PBS which won Emmy Awards. In 1984 he was production manager for Coca Cola's "Olympic Moment".

He has co-hosted programs on fine art with Robin (Rich and Famous) Leach and with Efrem Zimbalist Jnr. As a 'BBC TV interviewer' he duped Ned Beatty for "TV's Bloopers & Practical Jokes". He interviewed Hollywood celebrities, including "Dallas" producers and cast for German TV and, for French TV, Jane Russell and Cyd Charisse. He hosts medical programs like "Sexually Transmitted Diseases" and interviewed the Nation's top trial attorneys on "Law in America", a nationally syndicated series; he hosted the magazine series "Over 50" and "City on the Line", West Hollywood's phone-in show. He was network announcer and presenter for "World Access TV" and "Newsworthy". He hosted "The Naked Truth", a controversial program on the origins of religious beliefs, and, for Prime Ticket Sports Network, the series "Golf Video Magazine". During a 1990 stay in London, he was a news anchor/writer for Europe's Sky Television. Currently, he hosts "Home View Magazine", is national spokesman for Cable Vision Industries and has anchored the pilot for "The Planet Central TV Network", a new environmental channel for Worldview International.

As a corporate spokesman, he works on-camera in French, Italian, German, Spanish, English and, a program he narrated in 'American' English, won a National Telly Award in 1993. His clients include: Walt Disney, Bank of America, Coca Cola, Warner Brothers, McDonnell Douglas, American Red Cross, Mercedes Benz, British Aerospace and Jaguar.

As a businessman, he was elected a Fellow of the British Institute of Directors in 1961; he was managing director of Partridge & Wilcox Landscaping, Conservation Tools & Technology, a director of Heritage World Travel and he founded the Cinema Translation Center in Rome. He was European PR Consultant to Eley Ammuniton, Nitro Nobel of Sweden and Winchester UK.

His hobby is clay target shooting; he has also coached international trap and skeet shooters and instructors in several countries. In 1973 he was Gold Medalist and set a world record at the Nordic Championships. He was a member of the British International Shooting Team in the 70's and Chairman of the British International Shooting Board. In the 80's he won several California and West Coast International trap titles. In 1991 he again shot for Great Britain at the World Championships in Portugal. He has written books and over 100 articles, as European Editor and photographer for various American, English and European shooting magazines.

Derek's work as an actor includes the award-winning film "King and Country" with Dirk Bogarde, "McGuire Go Home" again with Bogarde, "Where the Spies Are" with David Niven, "Thunderball" (he was twice considered for the Bond role) and some Spaghetti Westerns. On TV he has appeared in "Star Trek", "Murder, She Wrote", "Remington Steele", "Hunter", "T. J. Hooker", "Call to Glory" and "Divorce Court". He starred as the villainous mercenary opposite Jack Palance (playing the 'good guy') in "The Ivory Ape" and he played himself, as a BBC TV news anchor on "Dallas".

With so much happening in his life, Derek remains a quietly-spoken, relaxed and charming man who has been described as "super-cool". Perhaps one of his philosophies for life sums it up best: "I discovered long ago," he says, "that it was much more fun to stay a kid at heart!"

This was originally written in 1980 by Michael Dalling, now Managing Director of the prestigious PR firm, Rogers and Cowan International, and subsequently updated for this book.

* * *

* The Head of Programmes and Production for Rhodesian TV, wrote this about Derek:

"Through every aspect of his work, Derek has achieved more – in his time here – for the Nation's morale than any other TV personality. The morale boost, that his sincerity and concern for Rhodesia, has brought to Rhodesians of all races, ages and in all walks of life, is remarkable. He has a fan mail following that I have not seen in all my nine years here and is perhaps the most professional personality Rhodesian TV has enjoyed in its ranks for many years. He is one of the finest people that I have ever had occasion to work with."

– Mike Hart-Jones, Salisbury 1978

BEFORE THE BOOK . . .

This book owes its existence to four individuals, while its contents are a reflection of the thoughts of hundreds of people, the world over. The four are: Daniel Posen, Rudyard Kipling, Jim Stephenson and Saint Francis of Assisi. Although a seemingly motley crew, the threads that bind them together formed the writer and so his words.

Daniel Posen was my dentist in New York. When I was five, he gave me a copy of Rudyard Kipling's *IF,* knowing Kipling to have been a friend of my father. I still have that copy. It has been with me on every desk throughout my lifelong travels and has always been engraved in my mind. I regard it as an ideal towards which everyone could strive to fashion himself. That any perfection is impossible to attain, in no way diminishes the importance of continually striving to reach it.

IF

If you can keep your head when all about you
    Are losing theirs and blaming it on you;
If you can trust yourself when all men doubt you,
    But make allowance for their doubting too;
If you can wait and not be tired by waiting,
    Or being lied about, don't deal in lies,
Or being hated don't give way to hating
    And yet don't look too good, nor talk too wise;

If you can dream and not make dreams your master;
   If you can think and not make thoughts your aim;
If you can meet with Triumph and Disaster
   And treat those two impostors just the same;
If you can bear to hear the truth you've spoken
   Twisted by knaves to make a trap for fools,
Or watch the things you gave your life to, broken,
   And stoop and build 'em up with worn-out tools;

If you can make one heap of all your winnings
   And risk it on one turn of pitch-and-toss,
And lose, and start again at your beginnings
   And never breathe a word about your loss;
If you can force your heart and nerve and sinew
   To serve your turn long after they are gone,
And so hold on when there is nothing in you
   Except the Will which says to them: "Hold on!"

If you can talk with crowds and keep your virtue,
   Or walk with Kings — nor lose the common touch,
If neither foes nor loving friends can hurt you,
   If all men count with you, but none too much;
If you can fill the unforgiving minute
   With sixty seconds' worth of distance run,
Yours is the Earth and everything that's in it,
   And — which is more — you'll be a Man, my son.

(*IF* is reproduced from *REWARDS AND FAIRIES* by Rudyard Kipling, by kind permission of Mrs. George Bambridge, Macmillan & Co. Ltd. and Doubleday & Co. Inc.)

Life: one-way traffic to a stop sign

Time passes as quickly or as slowly as we let it — it's up to us how, and how much we fill the one-way moments of a lifetime.

The happiness seed

Somewhere in any moment of happiness may lie the seed of its further growth, but it's not always easy either to recognize it or to nurture its development.

The unburdened tree

Memories of people, things, activities, which once filled our every moment, which no longer do and may never again: such is the pageant of changes which comprise the growth and development of living. And, just as sometimes a tree will grow the better for a little pruning of branches which have served their purpose, so must certain people and things fade from the scene of our current activities, so that we may grow, unfettered by bearing the burdens of the past.

Time

How can we ever treat the passing minutes so casually and off-handedly, that they slip by, unnoticed, into hours, days and then years? Our lives slip away as subtly but surely as the sand which runs through the narrow neck of the hour glass. One day we stop and look — and find there are more spent grains in the bottom than fresh ones waiting at the top.

A child lets sand run through his fingers: with equal casualness, many drop-outs from life, frequent street-corners, bars, and beaches while *their* sands run out, with so little to show for their passing. The only mark some of them will leave on this world, is where their feet have scuffed the sidewalk or the equally imperceptible mark on the bar they leaned against. *How do you fill an empty person?*

Timekeeping — or is it losing?

How kindly time adjusts its own clock within us: we still talk of yester*day's* memories — when they're already yester*year's.*

Now . . . and then

In the emptiness or unhappiness of today, we turn to our yesterdays for solace and security, or to our tomorrows for hope and promise. . . . for the past, being known, offers security — while the future, being unknown, looms as a frightening new adventure, fraught with menacing pitfalls. The solution is to delete the 'frightening' and then embark on the new adventure with courage, in the spirit of discovery and excitement.

Random jottings.

The prerogative of choice usually carries the obligation of responsibility.

* * *

The essence of beauty is simplicity. How simple is the beauty of life — and how complex its ugliness.

* * *

Enthusiasm is the most contagious of all non-toxic diseases' and it is a pure joy to watch the spread of this benign epidemic.

* * *

Every eye should know tears — but none too many. Every heart should know pain — but none too much.

* * *

Doing nothing is the most tiring 'activity' a person can indulge in.

* * *

Ignorance always speaks loudest.

Violence — the Creator's creation? . . .

Why is not only violence, but also the enjoyment of it, so deeply ingrained in man's intrinsic nature, even from childhood, that it appears almost impossible to exorcize it? *. . . and answer came there none.* But its *destructive* savagery seems to make a mockery of what is called His *Creation.*

. . . or man's?

There is a theory that many adults' indifference to violence — both in inflicting it and condoning its infliction on children, animals and other adults — stems from comic books and cartoon movies. They constantly portray the above being subjected to the most appalling kinds of violence: pushed off buildings and cliffs, steam-roller-flattened, burned, shot (complete with holes), dismembered, cut in half, decapitated, pulled apart, drowned, electrocuted, poisoned, gassed.

The variety is endless, but the conclusion always identical: within a couple of frames, the character recovers completely, totally unaffected by the violence it's been subjected to. If children's minds are so conditioned to the inconsequential ineffectiveness of violence, is it any wonder that some proportion of them will mete it out, both as children and adults, without ever considering that their actions could have *real* consequences?

More random jottings

Man clings to life as a flame clings to a wick when threatened by the wind, for the spark of life is so easily extinguished.

* * *

Thought knows no boundaries, until expressed in words, written or spoken, when it can lose its freedom to some men's fear of truth and progress.

* * *

Some 'modern thinking' considers that any 'old' idea must be outdated and worthless, while any 'new' idea must be good. Old ideas, tried and having passed the test of time, can still be valid despite their age, while new ideas *may* be . . . but not simply because of their novelty.

* * *

Growing up is when a puppy, following centuries of inbred instinct, lifts its leg for the first time . . . and falls over!

* * *

The most valuable endowment nature can make to any person, is to equip him with common sense. It does not seem to be a quality that can be acquired subsequently and the gap between academic or technical intelligence and common sense can be an awesome chasm.

* * *

Some people walk as if they have somewhere to go and a purpose for going there. Others walk as if they were going nowhere in particular and have even given up all hope of ever getting anywhere.

* * *

A teacher must be able to say and demonstrate the same facts and theories in a variety of different ways — until he finds the key which unlocks each individual's understanding.

* * *

Conscience: conditioned inhibitions.

* * *

"To make a long story short . . ." – isn't it amazing how adept some people are at making a short story long?

* * *

Shouldn't the art of communication be the ability to clearly convey a maximum of information, using a minimum of words? Yet many radio DJs manage to convey a minimum of information, using a maximum of words, as they spew out inane and inconsequential verbiage.

* * *

Many disappointments make up a dream fulfilled.

* * *

At times, the 'best looking' person can not only look ugly to himself, but even to others – while the 'ugliest' can look positively beautiful. It all depends on the beauty – or ugliness – inside

* * *

People who are impressed by appearances, deserve to be deceived by them.

* * *

Good luck could be described as having the ability to recognize, and so take advantage of, the fortuitous circumstances which capricious fortune places us in – as and when her whim so dictates.

* * *

Would it be reasonable to refer to a transsexual as a change of corporate image?

Discipline too, will be reaped as it is sowed

Unless we have *just* discipline applied to us by parents and teachers, during our childhood, how can we possibly be expected to apply *self-*discipline in our adolescent and adult years? Discipline would then be a most unwelcome stranger. However, without self-discipline, anyone is lost, of little use to himself or anyone else. Indulgent permissiveness is the greatest disservice parents can mistakenly lavish on their impressionable offspring. Self-discipline should usually result from the application of just discipline, but even more certainly will self-destruction be the offspring of permissiveness.

Belated charity — the great conscience cleanser

As many rich people's meeting with their maker becomes more imminent, they do a gradual about-face and start giving back (via sometimes questionable charities) the money they've made — by sometimes questionable means — to the improverished masses. Naturally, they make sure it's tax exempt.

Con Men

The skill of the confidence man is so simple that it can be divided into three stereotype stages: 1. He listens to you express your hopes, fears and desires. 2. As faithfully as a tape recorder, he then feeds you back promises of exactly what he now knows you want to hear. 3. When, after a while, you begin to have doubts as nothing materializes, he succeeds in coming up with *con*vincing reasons, as to why things aren't working out *exactly* as expected. This way, he can keep you on a string indefinitely, as *you* never want to sever the string which *you* still want to believe will turn out to be a golden thread — the very belief he so graciously, charmingly and oh, so easily caters to.

What often distinguishes the con man from the legitimate businessman — assuming each to be equally endowed with qualities of charm and graceful persuasion — is the con man's lack of attention to meticulous detail. That represents far too much trouble for him and would make his life unbearably tedious. But it's also how you can detect him and catch him out . . . IF you can take off the rose-colored spectacles for long enough to view him in his true light, instead of playing into his hands by glossing over his 'unimportant' (important), 'little' (big), 'oversights' (discrepancies) — because you so desperately want it to appear that way.

* * *

Oh for the clarity of hindsight — beforehand!

Further random jottings

Understanding a problem is the first step towards its constructive correction, and a small nucleus of people, infecting others with positive ideas and actions can, in time, change notions . . . and nations.

* * *

O.K., so you're usually right — just don't be so damned obvious about it!

* * *

Good advertising can persuade people to buy something once. If the product is good, it's all you have to do. If it's bad, it's all you'll be able to do.

* * *

A jack-of-all-trades is supposed to learn less and less about more and more and so should end up knowing nothing about everything. By the same token, a specialist must then be someone who learns more and more about less and less — and ends up knowing everything about nothing.

* * *

The climate of the weather, wherever we happen to be, is far less important than the climate of the people.

* * *

In every anticipated situation that faces us in life, somewhere between the wildest pipe dreams of our exuberant optimism and the most dreaded forebodings of our blackest pessimism — lies its reality.

Accidents

People always think they happen to *someone else* and never realize that in the impersonal world of statistics, *they* are just as likely to be that *someone else* — as any other person!

That warped prankster — Fate

Fate's somewhat ironic sense of humor decrees that some people get what they want, but don't necessarily deserve — while others get what they deserve — and almost certainly don't want!

Natural enemies . . .

is an expression all too frequently used; why do we not hear 'natural friends'? Years of inbred, but no longer relevant conditioning cause the cat to regard the dog as a natural enemy. So a cat will attack a puppy — who has yet to realize that a cat is supposed to be its natural enemy — and who just wants to play with what to him is a new-found friend in his world of daily new discoveries. But when puppies and kittens grow up in the same household, natural enmity gives way to natural friendship. How many analogies can be drawn for certain other natural enemies in nature's kingdom — and, among the supposedly reasoning races of man's world? Ever watched black and white kids playing together?

Kids

One of the greatest 'crimes' a child can commit, is to be different. It leads to total exclusion and isolation from the rest, who, in turn, will 'gang up' on the differing offender.

* * *

One of most children's basic rules of life: rules — adult version — are made to be broken. It's all part of the eternal war games between freedom-loving youth and restriction-imposing adult authority.

* * *

The day a child accepts that the age and experience of his parents might just give them a fighting chance of occasionally being right — is a major step in growing up.

* * *

How often do we hear an adult (ourselves?) describing a child as: "That ——— brat!" Can memory really fade so soon from yesterday's, or even yesteryear's 'brat'?

Youth's open road

You've probably noticed children waving to you from the back of a car or bus, but you don't often see an adult doing so. Kids have a basic, friendly, open desire for contact and communication with their fellow human beings — and haven't yet learned to be afraid of expressing it.

The age of discrimination

Great as the differences are between them, children seem to discriminate far less against adults, than vice versa.

The un-bilical cord

A mother sent an exasperated note to her son: "If only you could regard me as a woman, not as a mother . . ." By return came the *cri de coeur:* "Fine — if you'll treat me as a man, not as a son . . ."

Advanced, normal and backward

Often we hear a child described as being: "Very advanced for his age in some ways and quite backward in others". It rarely seems to occur to them that the child may just be normal in 'other ways' and not 'backward', in comparison to the ways in which he is 'advanced'.

Gang bravado

Several inferiority complexes banded together out of mutual fear, which add up to one very obnoxious and frequently aggressive collective ego.

* * *

People have a lot in common with the cactus — bristling, protective outsides and soft, defenseless insides.

Selfish business — selfless art

What some businessmen create is mostly for themselves. It is often at the expense or exploitation of others, with some almost incidental overspill of employment, by way of the employees contributing to what the businessmen are basically creating for themselves only: money, power and position.

Most artists (in the widest sense of the term) create basically to give enjoyment to others. Naturally they derive a sense of satisfaction and achievement for themselves — but at no one else's expense. Rarely — in the true artist — is the work performed primarily for commercial considerations.

"All that glitters . . ." — is just glitter

The ultimate irony of man's materialistic greed must surely be gold. With a tremendous expenditure of energy, human resources and risk to life and limb, man digs out of the bowels of the earth — where it is guarded by nature — a fairly useless metal. Further energy and resources are then expended in refining it. Once this lengthy and costly process is completed, another huge hole is dug (eg: Fort Knox) and the refined metal put back into the earth — where it is now guarded by man. The ultimate irony really is that approximately 80 per cent of all the gold now reposing in vaults has no *official* value — now that money is no longer based on the gold standard.

The hypocritic oath

When one reads of sick people and even emergency cases being turned away from some hospitals, for lack of proof of ability to pay, one wonders if some doctors' oaths are more hypocritic(al) than Hippocratic.

Enforced national dishonesty

The economic and taxation policies of many governments make it very hard for the average citizen to remain honest. Instead, he is almost obliged to cheat, lie and deceive — merely in order to retain enough of what he has earned to maintain a reasonable standard of living, rather than just a level of existence.

Some jobs

Pills of forgetfulness, whose effects last precisely from 9 to 5.

Beauty and the (Business) Beast

Although almost equal numbers of boys and girls are purely physically attractive, the same is not true of adults, where physically attractive women outnumber men. Why? Faces eloquently reflect what has gone on inside our minds. What some men are either obliged to do or choose to do in their pursuit of power and money, etches itself there with indelible ugliness.

Life's plowshare — self-inflicted

To stay young-looking and thinking, we must have internal peace and fulfilment. Turmoil and frustration not only eat out our insides, but etch their aging furrows deep into our faces.

The distorted reflection of intoxication

Some people drink so much that they not only lose control of themselves, but also think they're the wittiest, most intelligent people in the group. If they could see how pathetically stupid they really look, from then on, most of them would drink only as much as they could handle and still retain control of themselves.

Really — Raleigh!

Would you ever roll up some old, dead leaves, stick them in your mouth and set fire to them? "Of course not!" Well, it's good to hear you don't smoke . . .

Tasteless acquisition of the unnatural

Alcohol and tobacco are often referred to as 'acquired tastes' . . . how many people have lived to rue the day they 'acquired' them? Their acquisition is rarely even a matter of taste, but more often of expediency for business or social purposes, so as not to be 'left out' or 'different'. It is a sad commentary on 'accepted' social behavior that the non-smoker and non-drinker — who have only remained true to their *natural* tastes — are considered and 'put-down' as the odd-ones-out, instead of vice versa. However, there is now a growing trend to regard the 'nons' as the accepted, normal ones.

Health nuts

Another fashionable put-down is: "You're not one of those health food nuts?" If not a fanatic devotee of what can become an exaggerated cult, one can respond by asking innocently: "Oh, I suppose then you must be one of those ill health nuts?" What is wrong about taking reasonable care of one's health through the important factor of diet? The consequences of not doing so are most apparent all around. They are painful enough to observe — how much more so must they be to have to live with?

Calculation

Is it really more admirable in a man and more despicable in a woman? If so, why? Possibly another aspect of male influence and self-bias in setting 'accepted' behavior patterns.

Loneliness — or solitude?

"Lonely Are The Brave" — are they? Solitude should never be confused with loneliness — the former is a voluntary state.

Instant compatibility

You can know some people more deeply in five minutes than others you have 'known' for five years. Why and how? Having compatible astrological signs has always proved true for me. Carry-over from a previous incarnation is going into the realms of possible, but unprovable fantasy. The fact remains that there is an uncannily strong, same wave-length communication instantly established between some people. Equally certainly, there are others with whom one could spend an eternity without ever feeling comfortable, or even wanting to communicate.

Responsible communication

When someone ends a sentence with: "You know what I mean . . ." (often the insignia of New York cab drivers!): what they are saying is that they haven't the remotest idea what they mean and are desperately hoping that you will, so as to absolve themselves of the responsibility of getting themselves out of whatever they had started to get themselves into! Sometimes I can't resist answering with a callously naive "No?", for the only way they are ever going to learn to communicate fully with other people is by being obliged to undertake the responsibility of expressing themselves — by themselves.

5 down — 1 495 to go!

As communication and fostering it among others is one of my aims in life, I equipped myself with five languages. However, that still leaves me approximately 1 495 other languages I don't know! So I am no stranger to the depressingly helpless feeling of being cut off from people within touching distance. This enables me to readily understand the frustration of people who do not have the gift of expressing themselves easily — for I am unable to express myself, in other languages, with the same ease as in my native tongue. It's the same feeling: knowing in your mind what you want to say, but being unable to put it into words to convey the thought to someone else.

Communication — as she is spoke or writ

However, when someone wistfully expresses a desire to be able to write, I ask, seemingly facetious: "Can you talk?" Following their indignant affirmative, I explain that writing is simply transferring or putting down the spoken word on to paper. I never 'learned' to write, except by writing letters, which almost everyone does to family, friends and business associates. Just as with letters, the majority of spoken communication is on a one-to-one basis, and so is the majority of written matter read by one person at a time — a direct and very personal communication link. It really is as simple as the writer 'talking' — via the medium of the pen or typewriter — to the reader.

It's the same when working in television and 'talking to camera'. You are speaking to one or two people in the privacy of their homes — that the homes (or readers) may number in thousands or millions, should in no way affect the basic one-to-one communication between the presenter and each individual viewer . . . or reader.

Written matter should, ideally, neither insult the intelligence of the better educated, nor fail to reach the lesser-educated. Writers who deliberately use long, obscure words just to show how clever they are, defeat the whole purpose of communication: the simple sharing of ideas and information with *all* people. With my own writing, I attempt — by reading aloud — to ensure that generally the written words come across just as if I was speaking to someone.

I also bear in mind Churchill's advice on the use of short words and, always in front of me on my typewriter is the following passage: "Put it before them briefly so they will read it, clearly so they will appreciate it, picturesquely so they will remember it and, above all, accurately so they will be guided by its light."

Irrational distortion

It's astounding, the totally irrational fear some people — especially many women — have of small animals and even tinier insects. If that's the way they react to creatures so small and almost always quite harmless — how might they react to the appearance of some horrendous creature, as proportionally larger than themselves as they are to the tiny creatures? If anyone has the right to be petrified, surely it is the little creatures, whose lives can be extinguished by one deliberate or careless move on the part of the 'terrified', monster human being.

Rational distortion

We look in magazines and laugh at caricature drawings. Then one day we see that caricature walking down the street — and stop laughing. Life can play some cruel tricks on people, but people seem to have an even greater capacity for distorting themselves, by their ways of living.

Civilization:

a thin veneer, acquired over the ages, which can be stripped away in seconds to expose the baser elements of human nature. One of civilization's basest inventions: the bomb, can also destroy in seconds what it took centuries to create.

Thoughts on tears — the well-spring of the spirit?

We should all learn the value of tears and never feel ashamed of them. After all, what are they but the manifestation of the opposite emotion to the one which makes us smile — although they can express happiness too. Tears are often considered the province of women, but a discerning woman will realize that it can sometimes take a real man to cry. Never hold back tears — unless there's a very good reason for doing so — or you'll only get up-tight, bottle it up and blow up another time. Ideally, when you feel, whatever you feel — show it.

Tears

A child cries when young and hurt at play; a baby cries when younger and cannot have its way. Adults cry in pain, anger, fear or frustration — but the most beautiful tears are those of happiness or, for people who achieve greatness, especially in the face of adversity.

* * *

A mother's tears when she loses her daughter in marriage — or her son in battle.

* * *

Among the saddest tears — those which show, but never come from an animal's eyes ... and ... the eloquent, uncried tears of people, who have seen or experienced too much pain and hurt, to be able to cry any more ...

Ecological crimes

In the past, man committed many ecological crimes within the broad scope of: excessive depletion of natural resources without replacement; direct destruction of wildlife and its habitats; indirect destruction of the same (and ourselves) by a myriad of pollutants. He did so mainly through ignorance. Tragically, most are irreversible.

Today, no executives (and few individuals) can claim ignorance of the destructive effects of their corporate actions. That they continue to commit the same crimes, forces one to the inescapable conclusion that they do so for one reason: indiscriminately inconsiderate commercial gain. It is small consolation that the perpetrators of these outrages against nature and humanity condemn themselves to the same (not so) long-term fate as the rest of us — for their short-term profit.

A more recent ecological crime is over-producing people. Even this has commercial overtones. Every new baby represents another consumer ... which lights up dollar signs in the eyes of marketing men.

Consumption is a disease the wastes the human body. The addiction to worshipping the Almighty Buck at the altar of the great god Consumer, does the same to the body of any country.

Ecological jottings

In forests, as yet untouched by man's destructive hand, all creatures live out their perfect harmony, undisrupted and unsullied by nature's black sheep: an intruder described as *sapiens.* How sadly often has that so-called wisdom become perverted and destructive.

* * *

One reads of the proud achievements of those who have 'reclaimed' land — perhaps without considering the resultant destruction of vital elements in the complex, delicate and inter-dependent ecological structure.

* * *

Man's too simple means of entering this world is fast becoming an equally easy passport into the next, as he persists in over-breeding himself out of existence. His wondrous creation is growing into his horrendous self-destruction.

* * *

"Make love, not babies" is a pertinent and timely slogan. It is also an admirable and essential attitude for resolving today's acute overpopulation problem.

* * *

Man — one of the world's most easily renewable resources, but the least easily supportable.

* * *

Some artists' impressions try to improve on nature . . . and fail. Most industries' 'impressions' *don't* try to improve . . . and are far more successful.

* * *

Every time journalists (such as I) write articles and a paper publishes say a million and a half copies — 4 000 trees have to die to print them . . . ouch!

* * *

Tranquility is a golden sunset, mirrored in a lake, punctuated by swallows and crowned with lazily drifting clouds.

* * *

Perfection is a leaf, a snowflake, a crystal . . . perfection is a feather, a sea shell, a butterfly's wing . . . perfection is an eagle's soar, a cat's prowl, a salmon's leap . . . perfection is spring's green, autumn's gold, winter's white . . . perfection . . . is all of nature . . . *let's keep it that way.*

Ecology — a new religion?

Religions could make quite a case for a Creator through a study of ecology (the inter-relationship of all aspects of nature). Before man entered the scene — and started changing it — some*one* (?) had the whole intricate scheme beautifully planned. It's hard to see where man fits in. Allowing him to 'develop' so far may have been *his* one mistake. Could be why *he* doesn't make *his* presence felt much nowadays!

The power of life and death

To kill birds and animals for the protection of crops (when all other means have proved ineffective), to kill to protect one's life or to eat is one matter, but to kill for *the pure pleasure of killing* — and call it a sport . . . each person must satisfy his own conscience. One fact should be too obvious to mention, but still seems to need pointing out: the 'game little sporting bird or animal' does not willingly offer its life in the interests of sport, the decision is the sportsman's — the creature has no choice. I seriously question our 'right' to take life for no better reason than to derive pleasure from it — seems a pretty morbid way to enjoy oneself.

* * *

Few people even think twice before deliberately killing a spider caught in the bath or carelessly extinguishing the life of an ant under a misplaced foot. Obviously we can't watch every step, but millions of tiny, *harmless* creatures are killed through irrational fear, easily avoidable carelessness, or, by those sadly warped specimens of humanity who delight in senseless killing.

The collectors of death

Other people derive pleasure from collecting dead creatures. They range from butterfly collectors and fur-laden women to big-game hunters. I used to number in their ranks, but after it became obvious that life was infinitely more beautiful than death, I did my 'collecting' with a camera. *Some* big-game hunters have ego problems. One way they can prove what big, brave he-men they are is by killing 'ferocious' (provoked) or 'docile' (petrified) animals, placed in their sights by professional hunters — who also protect their fearless clients from the perils of faulty marksmanship.

Culling, when there is an excess of game in an area, has to be acceptable, but usually the need to deal with the imbalance has been created by man's interference upsetting nature's carefully calculated balance.

* * *

(When I was younger, I killed many birds and animals officially classified as pests or vermin by the British Ministry of Agriculture. Although I immensely enjoyed being outdoors, studying and pitting my wits against the instincts of wild creatures, I never enjoyed the killing. Even from the day I started, I knew that one day I would kill no more – except to eat, or to protect crops, but certainly not for pleasure. That day came eighteen years ago and since, it's been only targets and clay pigeons. I've handled firearms for about 30 years, becoming expert with some, proficient with all, including the use of handguns, rifles and shotguns for self-defence. As Chairman of the British International Shooting Board and a member of the British Team, the above views are not those of the occasionally hysterical, frequently uninformed anti-blood sports brigade.)

Life and death in nature

As a general rule — with few exceptions — nature's creatures only kill for food, as and when it is needed, or for survival. Very few species kill for pleasure — as man does — even fewer wantonly — as man does — and none for commercial gain!

The sure way to end all wars — for ever

Although I served as a Radar Officer in the Royal Air Force, I dislike — in a purely idealistic sense — the base cause of things military, because, of all man's stupidities, destruction of one's own kind is the most stupid, and, practiced virtually only by men. Of course, the defense of one's country against unprovoked attack is justifiable, but most wars have been started by greedy rulers, politicians, religious fanatics or terrorists — who rarely risked their lives in the killing they initiated. If military service for the world's armed forces was restricted to those *over* the age of fifty, the major international war games would promptly cease to exist.

Anti-military 'soldiers'

It's ironic that among the younger 'with-it' set are some of the most vociferous anti-militarists — who parade around, adorned in surplus or pseudo-military uniforms and insignia.

Reincarnation:

I am inclined to believe in the possibility of some form of reincarnation. The limitations of my human mind can find no other acceptable explanation for certain facts I have observed, others I have read about and even some factors in myself. To illustrate the point, an extreme example: child geniuses, playing the classics or doing higher calculus at the age of four or five. A study of parental lineage dismisses the possibility of the knowledge being inherited. It is also certain that they didn't have time to *learn* their extraordinary degrees of skill in a couple of years — the standards they often attain, usually take the best part of a full lifetime — for 'normal' people.

Where did the skills come from? The only half-way reasonable explanation to me, is that they were the result of another existence or existences. The following example illustrates the point: a four year-old Negro infant prodigy could perform the most complex maneuvers on a set of drums, far in excess of almost all existing professional drummers. I watched him play; the sounds he produced were magnificent, his manual dexterity unbelievable. However, the most remarkable aspect was the child's *total detachment.* He looked dumb and bored, and stared vacantly around with his mouth open, as if totally divorced from what his hands compelled him to do.

In my early teens, I would be discussing fairly deep aspects of psychology and behavior patterns which startled adults, who would ask if I had been reading Professor so-and-so. I always had to admit ignorance of the existence of these learned experts. It seemed that I (and many like me) had come into the world with a store of information and knowledge about subjects with which we had never had the slightest contact. The sequel to these experiences is perhaps revealing.

As I became exposed to various facets of life, I found my experiences of people and their behavior tied up with what I had already instinctively known about them — but *before* I had had any practical experience on which to base these inbuilt theories. So, until someone produces a more acceptable-to-the-limitations-of-the-human-mind theory to explain where the knowledge came from, I will continue to believe in the possibility of reincarnation.

Soul and death:

Webster's dictionary defines 'soul' as: "The spiritual, non-material part of man's being; the immortal part, that which survives after the death of the body". I wonder who their source of information was to enable them to be so categorically sure about it surviving after death? I don't know if I have a soul and no one could ever prove that I, or he, does. But, if I equate soul with mind, a "non-material part" which I know I have, it can make sense.

When the body is asleep, it is, apart from the reduced activity of the vital organs, in the nearest comparable state to death. In this condition, however, the *mind* is free to wander the known world and another world of fantasy (?) — sometimes aimlessly and sometimes with direction. Could it not be a reasonable assumption and acceptable within the limitations of our comprehension, that this is exactly what happens at death? The mind /soul once more departs its temporary housing, just as it can do each night, only this time it doesn't return . . . Where does it go?

Academic learning — or the school of Life?

It's usually better to learn firsthand for ourselves — whenever possible — rather than by listening to a second party telling us about third parties' experiences.

Those who try to be most 'with it' . . . are generally most 'without it'.

A worry is only as big . . . as we let it be . . . and happiness . . . is just a smile away.

2

LIVING WITH ONESELF

The ability to live with oneself is the prime requisite of any happy and successful life.

The game of life

Life is a matter of moments and each one should be lived as it comes along. Enjoy the good ones to the full and make the best of the inevitable bad ones. We cannot totally control our destinies and the most acceptable premise I have found is this: life is like a deck of cards; fate deals us the hand — but it is up to us how we play the cards.

Rules of life — simplified!

Find out who you are — be it. Decide what you want to do — do it.

Control your own fate . . .

In life, we've only one time round. If we don't get what we want out of it, we've generally only ourselves to blame, for most of us have the right of choice in all matters and decisions — *originally,* at least.

. . . and conscience

If we do nothing we're ashamed of, we shouldn't have to hide anything or have any secrets. We would then never need live in fear of anyone exposing something about us. Life can be a lot simpler than people make it. The choice, again, is in our own hands.

Crosses

Idealism, sincerity and integrity are tough crosses to bear through life, but immeasurably worth while — inside.

Perpetual renovation

Never be saddened by endings; they always herald beginnings — the episodic chapters of life.

The cocktail of eternal youth

So as not to grow old before our time, it's vital to retain the endearing qualities of youth: enthusiasm, curiosity, naive wonderment and an appreciation of the simple beauties that abound in life. If we can keep these qualities, along with youth's bewildering, unpredictable spells of impish madness, and successfully blend in wisdom, responsibility and sobriety, we will have a formidable combination to sustain a full and interesting life. The resultant 'elixir' will be the envy of yesteryear's alchemists, but, unlike them, we must always be ready to share it with others who are still open and receptive.

Split personalities

Many individuals have two people dwelling in them: deep down, the one they'd like to be — and on the surface, the one they've let life turn them into.

"Music hath charms . . ."

Many people find music great for 'getting in the mood' — any 'up' mood. Music can also be an irresistible remedy for getting oneself *out* of any 'down' mood.

Growing forwards — backwards

Some people have to grow older in order to lose enough inhibitions to become the youngsters they never were before. Some then have the pleasure of going through life growing ever younger, gaining knowledge and enjoying the freedom to exploit it to the full, for the benefit of themselves — and others.

Relax away your ulcers

Whenever we're in a situation we don't like, we have two choices: get out, or make the best of it — if the former is impossible. Many people follow a third course and end up with ulcers and premature gray hair from getting themselves worked up — negative thinking — which proves nothing and achieves less. A simple example is the traffic jam: *get out* of it by taking an alternate route. If you can't, there's no point in sitting there fuming and swearing, so *make the best of it:* listen to the radio, read the paper, or just relax. This positive attitude is particularly applicable to usefully filling any moments of enforced waiting — *for no moment has ever been known to return.*

'Never'

Ideally, the only time we should employ the term 'never' is to persuade ourselves *never* to use it again. This is an insurance policy of allowing for the changing circumstances and contingencies of life. We 'never' know when we might find ourselves in a situation where we should do something we once said we would 'never' do. Stubborn pride, in maintaining that self-imposed commitment, could prevent our taking a course of action which might be vital for the preservation or continuation of some important aspect of our lives. 'For ever' is another expression to be avoided.

Balance and moderation . . .

. . . of all aspects of life are major contributors to health, happiness and success. The main balance should be between work and recreation. Most moderation should be applied to the appetites of eating, drinking and sex. Each individual should, through experimentation, discover his own balance and moderation. *One man's excess is another's insufficiency and one man's perversion is another's normality.*

What goes down, must come up

I believe strongly in the compensation theory of life: for the lows of life, there are corresponding highs. I deliberately did not use the reverse order, for that is the sign of the pessimist. He never fully enjoys his ups, because he's already anticipating and therefore bringing on his next down. We don't have to try for them, they have a habit of looking after themselves! I also believe that to truly appreciate the exhilarating heights, we must have experienced the dismal depths. For those who want to avoid these depths, the drab doldrums of 'safe', gray mediocrity are the only alternative — the sort of life where nothing very terrible ever happens, but, by the same token, nothing very exciting either.

An unequal equality

All of us are born with roughly the same desires, hopes, wishes and fears, but not all, by a long way, are equally equipped to respectively fulfill and dispel them.

It's the same difference

What's different in life? People, ideas, places, jobs, hobbies and all their permutations. What's the same? Happiness and unhappiness, derived from them.

Enviable sacrifice

There's always someone who envies someone else's situation in life — without stopping to consider what lies behind it. We all have this choice: what do we want; what do we have to give up to get it; is it worth what must be given up? (I chose freedom, based on inner security — and gave up financial security).

Money . . . or achievement?

Does one simply make a good living, or risk the ups and downs of capricious fortune to someday become a somebody who leaves his mark on the world? For those who rate inner security more highly than material security, it is more important to try to do something worth while than merely to sell oneself for the highest fee.

Never, never give up hope . . .

for just around the corner, at the darkest moment, can be the fulfilment of a lifetime's dream. Typically, it can happen in the most unlikely circumstances, when not looking for it and when just about reconciled to not achieving it. Think how long some have waited . . . *Papillon* for one.

Inevitable?

Many people either willingly or 'unavoidably' give in to the 'inevitability' of an *existence* beyond their control, instead of fighting to make the *life* they really want. It's certainly easier and far more peaceful . . . superficially.

Know thyself . . .

We should study ourselves to know ourselves and our mannerisms, but with care, for we will be treading the fine line between the disasters of being self-conscious and the advantages of being conscious of self.

* * *

Before we try to find a companion in life — like a wife — it's a good idea to have found ourselves.

* * *

Being, some way or other — within reasonable (?) bounds of non-conformity — is probably better than being everyone else's way, and definitely preferable to being no way at all.

* * *

By the time some people learn who they are, they have become something they don't really like. So they spend the rest of their sad lives running away from themselves or hiding behind a facade of pretending to be what they are not.

. . . and like thyself

Occasionally, someone will say to me, with biting sarcasm, and ill-concealed jealousy: "Well, you like yourself, don't you?" My happy affirmative is not the reply they want and their reaction only sadly shows that they have yet to come to terms with themselves. My explanation that it took years of self-study to reach this happy state, only provokes their further reaction of: "Aren't you the all-time egotist, too!"

Life's most basic rule is that you must be able to live with yourself. To do this, you've got to like yourself. No one would willingly choose to spend an evening, let alone a lifetime, with someone he didn't like. We can always get away from other people, even close family, but never from ourselves. Sadly, many people try to, by cutting off their awareness of themselves in drink or drugs. This is negative, non-constructive escapism. They're always there to greet

themselves next morning with that S.O.B. of a hangover —
a hangover which is an accurate reflection of their
hang-ups. If the same time, effort and money were devoted
to constructing an individual who would be a pleasure to
live with, most of the mandatory 24 hours of all our days,
that would be progress instead of stagnation or regression.

We give out to others what we have inside us. If we like
ourselves (with humility, not conceit), we'll be happy and
will leave happiness with every person whose life we touch.
The reverse is just as true. When I feel depressed or
temporarily down, I avoid other people, having no wish to
inflict my miseries on them. Most of them probably have
enough of their own to cope with, without the extra burden
of mine.

When I feel good, I want everyone to share it and bask in
the sunny rays of my happiness. It's so rewarding to relieve
them of some of their worries. When we feel happy, we
have an almost supernatural power to absorb the sour wine
of other people's unhappiness, dissolve it in the distillery of
our own happiness and transform it into the bubbling,
heady champagne of the pure joy of being alive.

Servicing the mind.

The most generous, spiritual giver must sometimes
reverse roles and take. No one is a limitless cornucopia and
everyone needs replenishment before giving again. Just as
an engine runs on fuel, so every creature's body runs on the
fuel of food.

The mind also needs re-fueling and, as with the engine
and the body, regular maintenance and unabusive
treatment will prolong its useful, active life.

A 3 000 mile blood change and lubrication

Strange how many of us routinely service our cars . . . but
not our bodies.

An emotive bomb . . .

It's wonderful to be free enough to show our emotions. Some people just can't, no matter how much they want to. Something, maybe fear of being ridiculed or memory of past hurt, dries it up inside, or bottles it up — till one day it explodes, endangering the human bomb and all within range. Emotions, like a spirited horse, function best when held in check by a prudent rein. Although emotions should be given a free rein whenever possible, there are obviously times when it can be wrong to show them. However, there is no reason, for instance, not to cry when music, a film, a book, human achievement or sorrow moves one to. This nonsense that a man should be ashamed to show his emotions can be carried to ridiculous extremes.

. . . and an emotional whirlpool

Decisions made totally emotionally are generally neaded for equally total disaster. Moral: don't make decisions while under the influence of emotional intoxication. It is a piteous sight to see someone drowning in his own emotions. It is almost worse to watch others sucked into the vortex created by the drowning person, or pulled down with him as the straws he grasps at. Either we control our emotions — or they will ru(i)n us.

Unguided tours — local version

Travel the world at every possible opportunity — you never know whom you'll meet or what you'll learn. If you can't do it internationally, travel your own 'world' around you — wherever you are and however small you may consider it. The only thing you can be sure of by doing the reverse — sitting alone in your home — is that no one is going to come in and find you and nothing is going to happen. (I know, I've tried it).

The human reversal process

Ever noticed how we can look at a situation today, when we don't want to do it, and come up with a score of convincingly insurmountable obstacles for its rejection — and tomorrow, when we've changed our minds, how the obstacles float away like gossamer before the wind of our new-found ability to move mountains?

"Heer spiks one ingleesh"

There's a point we must reach to be successful in learning foreign languages, that can be applied to much in life: the point of losing our tightness and inhibitions so that we don't care about making mistakes. From that moment on, we are free to experiment and progress by learning from our mistakes — instead of being held back by the fear of making them.

An experienced anemone

Every experience or involvement in life contains a balance, or more likely, an imbalance, of benefit and hurt. We can isolate or insulate ourselves and be fairly sure of never being hurt, but then life becomes empty.

It takes courage to make ourselves vulnerable, to open our hearts and minds, and to say: "Life, here I am — let's live, not just exist." It's deeply worth while, but we must accept that sometimes life will hurt. Like the sea anemone, we'll pull in our bruised, sensitive feelers and withdraw into ourselves. Then, we should learn a lesson from the gentle anemone: if it didn't put out its feelers again, it would die from starvation and what's more, its feelers never harden. If *we* don't open ourselves again, we'll starve emotionally and if we become too hard, we'll never feel again.

No one *likes* to be hurt (masochists are excused from reading on!), but it is one of life's ways of maturing us. Being hurt is part of the game of life; it's called experience. Past experiences are life's bank of intangible assets. They can always be drawn on when the situation requires them. The fullest life is not necessarily the one exposed to most experiences, but the one enriched by drawing constructive lessons from their respective happiness and pain.

Purpose

When our lives, or even the most mundane act of living, have purpose, we give out positive vibrations which attract people and 'happenings'. When life, or any part of it, becomes aimless, negative vibrations result and both avoid us.

Hurts and disappointments

All of us have experienced them — just and unjust — in a bewildering variety of ways. We can let them become good reasons for convincing ourselves of the necessity to seek oblivion and escape from their reality — remembered or actual. But, rather than run away, we should surmount them and come through their ordeals as better people.

Mistakes

We all make them, otherwise how would we learn? The trick is not to repeat a mistake. That's *only* depressing and it can be a lot more fun making new ones! The only purpose of yesterday's mistakes is to make our todays and tomorrows better.

Regrets

We have to (and can) live with our mistakes — *no one is goof-proof* — but to have to live with the regret of not having done something, that can become intolerable. How many times have we heard someone (ourselves) saying: "If only I'd been . . . done . . . gone . . . etc. I might . . . could . . . would . . . have been etc."Go and do whatever it is and then rest in peace with the *certain* knowledge that it was right or wrong — and not the never-to-be-resolved *uncertainty* and its accompanying nagging doubts. That kind of regret can eat a person's heart out, and dejection can destroy not only today's efforts, but also the will for future achievement. So do it — no matter how many times you fall flat on your face and crawl away to lick your wounds. To bend a well-known saying: "It is better to have lived and erred, than never to have lived at all."

An 'experienced' afterthought

It takes strength of character to come through suffering or any of life's rougher experiences and not carry forever the open wounds of closed, bitter cynicism. Even though we may be scarred, we should always learn from them. To be untouched by them is ignorance and emptiness. However, it has been said that ignorance is bliss — the choice is ours.

Shut up and listen

Don't be afraid to display ignorance in a genuine and humble willingness to learn. Know-it-alls will never learn more. They never admit there could be something they don't already know, so who's going to tell them anything? It's always worth hearing things we already know — for the sake of picking up even one new item of knowledge. Besides, it's usually welcome to know that someone else has had the same experiences or has reached the same conclusions on a subject of mutual interest.

Goals — and reaching them

Most of us are destined to spend our lives working — and dreaming of leisure-time pursuits. This makes a strong case for doing a job that we really enjoy — one which brings us inner peace and contentment, even if it doesn't pay so well as another job. Often, one meets people doing jobs they dislike, but earning fabulous sums of money. They say (and believe) they are doing so to buy freedom and the ability to pursue altruistic or artistic goals. Some become so inextricably involved that they lose sight of their original purpose.

Others become mere worshippers of money and enslave their every hour to its accumulation. What use is money if we don't do something with it? A few attain their goal, only to find that due to their own development and changing circumstances over the years, the goal they once wanted no longer interests them. Others find that devoid of the achievement work gave them, they can't enjoy undiluted (unbalanced) recreation and leisure activities.

The cost of freedom

What price financial freedom? When financial security must be bought in bonded chains, the price is too high — (for me).

The little engine got off its butt and tried — how about you?

It's never occurred to me that there is anything I can't do, if I want to badly enough. But, even though Ian Fleming said: "The possible is not what you can do, but what you want to", there are undoubtedly areas I would be lost in! My attitude when faced with a new challenge is still: "I'll do it", rather than: "I wonder if I can?" I believe that with the will to succeed, applied common sense and a degree of technical ability — acquired by falling flat on one's face a few times and so having to learn practicality — there is damn little we can't achieve.

So much more would be open to all people, if only they'd apply this simple philosophy. Their lives would become more satisfying and fulfilled. The world is full of a million fascinating things to do and learn. Next time, instead of gazing admiringly and enviously at someone doing something and assuming you can't do it, get off your butt and try! Remember the little engine that worked its way up the giant hill, puffing: "I think I can, I think I can . . ." and roared down the other side with a triumphant: "I knew I could, I knew I could!!"

Don't climb backwards . . .

In life there are always greater goals to be attained, greater challenges to be met. Never make the mistake of assuming you are 'there' — that's only one step away from slipping backwards. The higher we get, the greater the danger, as on the ascent of any 'mountain' — of life or reality.

... but, "Know thyself"

Success creates pressures to do more and better. However, it is preferable that the motivation to do so comes from within ourselves and not from the expectancy of others — provided we know our own limitations and how to gradually expand them. Other people almost certainly do not and are more likely to try to make us expand too far, too fast (especially if they stand to benefit financially), with disastrous results. However, it is also true that some people do need outside stimulation. Just remember what the ancients said: 'Know thyself'.

'Dream' dreams and 'real' dreams

I have never been afraid to venture into the world of practical, anticipatory dreams, in spite of all advice to the contrary. When I have been told of a job, a trip, some pleasant event that *may* happen, I promptly indulge in graphic dreams and detailed plans about it. If it doesn't come off, I am rarely disappointed. I have already had a load of fun imagining it. Life has no vacuums, so something else must fill the place and time span allotted in one's mind/life for the cancelled event. It may be better, as good as or possibly not as good, but there certainly won't be a void. If the projected event does come off, have I spoiled my fun by anticipating it? Not a bit! I get double the pleasure, for reality will never be *exactly* like the dream! Another piece of life insurance I buy for myself — at no cost.

Forgetting and forgiving

Most of us, at times, especially during the early, groping years, will make bad judgements and mistakes. In time, people forget or are replaced by others not equipped with the memory of our growing pains. So don't be afraid to try again, besides, it's a big wide world!

* * *

To err is human, to forgive divine — but the best we can *expect* from other humans, is that they forget.

Posthumous artistic recognition?

The time-*honored (?)*, ritual pattern of the creative person's frustrated efforts to achieve recognition: at first, no one wants anything he produces — no matter how brilliant it may be. Later, so much later (sometimes too late), after some brave, far-sighted individual has given one of the creator's works the light of day and it's become successful, *they* suddenly want anything he's ever done — no matter how unworthy it may be.

To reach the unreachable star . . .

To believe utterly in the eventual success of all one has set out to do in life is important. It is equally important to spend life trying to fulfil the dream and never give up. Giving up invites irreversible regrets later in life. Just be damn sure the dream is at least potentially attainable!

Pond life

If you consider yourself a 'big fish', but find yourself temporarily without a big pond to swim in, you can always keep in shape in a little one, as the swimming's basically the same. But a little fish who becomes a big fish in a little pond, can still be a very small fry if he ever dares to enter a big pond. He can even be a very dead little fish, if he can't move fast enough to avoid the sharks on the other side of the dam.

Status symbols.

The only real 'status' is that which we carry within us and which manifests itself clearly and aggravatingly to those whose cars, clubs and bank accounts are *their* only status symbols.

Downers and uppers

We need self-discipline, self-control and confidence most, in two diametrically opposed situations. We need it when struggling through the lowest depths of empty depression — to hold ourselves together and to avoid remaining in that non-productive state by indulging in an orgy of wallowing in self-pity. Conversely, it is needed when 'everything couldn't be going better' — either to enable us to cope adequately with all that is happening, or to ensure that everything remains at its exhilarating level. At such heady heights, it is all too easy to slack off, start taking things for granted and spend too much time 'living it up'. Meanwhile, slightly neglected affairs can be starting the barely perceptible slide down — back to the former state from which we may have recently so laboriously climbed up.

It takes a great deal of self-knowledge to know when and how to relax the reins on oneself — but relaxed they must be, or we'll 'blow up' inside. Too much relaxation heralds the disastrous, retrogressive down-slide, while too little could head us on the equally disastrous route of tranquilizers and pep pills, ulcers and the psychiatrist's couch.

Fine lines . . .

There's a very fine line between efficiency and laziness. An efficient person sensibly tries to avoid doing superfluous or unessential work. But there are the times when, for example, we strain to reach an object that could have been reached with half the time and effort expended, if we'd gotten up to get it in the first place. That's generally what we end up doing — unless we're so stubborn that we'd rather fall out of bed or pull a muscle to prove our worthless point!

* * *

There's an equally fine, but rather more important line between genuinely proving something to our satisfaction and deluding ourselves by sycophantic rationalization.

. . . and sweeping generalizations

It's easier to be honest — if you can (financially) afford to be.

* * *

Honesty only frightens those who can't take it — or don't want to.

* * *

Vice is an excess of anything we enjoy to the point where it does us more harm than good.

Moral strength . . .

is the ability to be alone and not have to depend on anyone. Money can always be made in one way or another — emotional security cannot.

The unknown

It is often easier to face the most frightening, apparently insurmountable *known* problem, than an unknown one — which could turn out to be insignificant. The unknown produces a reaction of fear and a tendency (self-defensive?) to assume that it will be a lot worse than it usually is.

Hidden lights . . . and faults

To be unaware of a hidden talent, or a major character defect which holds us back in life, is a tragedy. To be aware of either, or both, and do nothing about them, is a crime — against ourselves and others.

Bridge insurance

People sometimes accuse me of 'crossing bridges before I come to them'. We all do a bit of that, but I construct bridges I may never use. It's another of my no-cost life insurance policies. Emergency situations occur in life which require split-second decisions. We can't prepare for all of them, but we can for some. He who is prepared has a better chance of making the right decision under stress, when there's little or no time for deliberation. So I build bridges which are solidly constructed for safe crossing, if and when needed. If they're never used, they do no harm, take up no space (the brain's storage capacity is unlimited) and may even cope with a similar situation for someone else.

Self-destruct buttons

The more we depend on anything outside our will power — like alcohol, cigarettes, pep-pills, tranquilizers and all the other drugs, from marijuana on downwards — the more we become slaves to it and the less we own ourselves. None of them offers more than a temporary solution to whatever it is we are running away from or propping ourselves up to face. Afterwards, we still have to face ourselves in our metaphorically naked state. The sight can be so distressing that another application of one of the above is required. The slippery downhill path is then further self-greased.

Drugged mental hardwear

To those who freak out and turn on: If you want to expand your minds, furnish them, but not with crutches — that's permanent tune out.

Analysis of a shape

In the proverbial final analysis, we can depend only on ourselves and if we can't do that, we're in pretty bad shape!

Telling lines

The lines on our faces don't lie. They show clearly whether we are basically happy or unhappy people. It takes no more effort to crease our faces into a smile than it does to frown. Every other facial mannerism, resulting from a repetitive internal reaction or feeling, will also etch its lines for all to read.

A distinguished leaf

There is always someone who is different — like the leaf that stubbornly clings to its branch when the others have fallen, and holds out till spring and the advent of new life. This is as Homer's quotation: "Always to be the best and distinguished above the rest."!

Tuition and stinct - preface with 'in'

Instinct should not be confused with intuition. Instinct is the reaction resulting from conditioned habits or reflexes. These can be centuries-old genetic inheritances, or the result of deliberate training, such as the evasive action 'instinctively' taken to avoid accidents by professional drivers. Intuition is that little voice that comes from who knows where — unasked — and is always right, even when we can find many logical reasons why it should be wrong, for logic is intuition's most destructive enemy.

Women easily (and often willingly) confuse or equate instinct and intuition with emotion. They will also override both — and logic too — when emotion dictates otherwise. This is why they get themselves involved in similarly unhappy love affairs, when past experiences warn them against making the same mistake!

The 'voice' of 'God'?

As long as we deny intuition and fight it with logic, it will remain a stranger to us. It's as if it were saying: "Why bother knocking myself out, trying to get through to this stubborn, ungrateful blockhead?" As soon as we accept that it exists and has an uncanny knack of *always* being correct — it will become a more frequent and welcome visitor. Could intuition be the means of communication from what we call 'God'?

Logic? — female version

When a woman 'can't afford' something, it's generally some dull, practical item which she (or the household) *needs,* but she doesn't *want.* When she 'can afford' something, it's probably some entirely unnecessary item, which she has no *need* for at all, but *wants.* She will then find some excellent, plausible justification for spending . . . the money she just saved on the *needed,* but *unwanted* article referred to above. The male of the species has also been known to exhibit the same behavior pattern!

Unhealthy pride

As a kid, I refused to admit that I could get ill. My reaction to any minor illness was of anger at the inconvenience caused and I would never go to a doctor if I could avoid it. The years instilled a little sense. Now, if something seems wrong, instead of worrying about it and maybe turning nothing into something serious, it's immediately: "Anything wrong, doc?". If there is: "Fix it, please", and if not, it's back to work and sleep with a freed, unworried mind. The stupidities immature pride can push us into!

Hurt

Most of us have known times when we have had to bury the hurt a little deeper inside and look a little braver on the outside.

Loneliness, emptiness and depression

They're not easy to face without the unstable props of drinking, smoking and drugs. It can tax self-control and confidence to their limits — and beyond. But, even when there's only the barest spark of light at the end of the long, dark tunnel, it's still better to hang on without the props.

Drip, drip . . .

All the achievements of past years can never fill the empty
24 hours of now. Although such a period may be but a drop
in the bucket of our time, beware — buckets fill up.

Yesteryear's depression . . .

I once wrote: "What happened to me today? I grew
another day older. What is the point of it all?"

. . . and today's antidote

No one has the right to be bored. A hundred lifetimes
would not suffice to even see all there is in this fantastic
world of land and under sea — let alone learn everything!
My only regret is that I am obliged to sleep sometimes —
what a waste of time!

Life begins *again* at 40

How often does one hear the sad lament: "If only I knew
then what I know now . . ." If you don't know something
about life by the time you're 40, you probably never will!
However, if you have remained young in body and outlook,
there's another whole lifetime ahead. Hence the above
amendment to the well-known expression.

Good looks . . .

a generally fortunate accident of birth, permitting one to view one's early morning reflection in the mirror with a little less displeasure than those less favored by chance.

. . . and conceit

Conceit could be defined as an erroneous or self-inflated belief in an ability that one doesn't have, or doesn't have to the extent one would have others — or oneself — believe. Vanity, when applied to looks, could be similarly described. Genuine self-confidence stems from a quiet belief in and grateful acceptance of real ability, perhaps enhanced by the fortunate bonus of looks.

People-watching and self-construction

We meet many people as we live. They are all worth studying. Depending on how well we succeed in assessing their true characters, we will be aware of the good and bad aspects of their personalities. The benefits of such observations are twofold. All knowledge of what makes people tick is invaluable in any dealings with them. Of greater value still is the way we can benefit ourselves even more personally.

When we see a constructive or positive quality we do not possess, we should endeavor to acquire it and mold it into our personality. When we observe the reflection of a destructive or negative characteristic, we should strive to eliminate it. Such priceless help in character-building is not available so cheaply elsewhere, but this source is free — to all who have insight.

"Timber!"

To be borne well in mind — especially if trying to implement any of the philosophies expounded here — is James Thurber's classic advice that it can sometimes be better to fall flat on one's face, rather than to lean over *too* far backwards.

My personal aims in life

As I grew, my life-effort shifted from collecting material objects, which certainly cannot be taken with me when I die, to the acquisition of these intangibles: knowledge, experience, and compassion through understanding. My aim is to present their composite, blended with entertainment, as a legacy of thought-provoking truth and happiness. This I can leave behind for others, and, who knows, I may be able to take it with me!

* * *

I choose to aim for achievement in life, rather than fame and fortune. Achievement will probably lead to fame and can be turned into fortune. To pursue only fame is a hollow quest, as all fame, even notoriety, must have its day of reckoning in public, but, far more important — years of reckoning in private. Fortune itself can never buy achievement and no more than a tawdry imitation of fame, based on the bought, fawning words of parasites.

Peace and war. (From a letter to one of my brothers in 1967)

"You query whether it may be me who is facing reality and the rest of the world that isn't. In some ways I believe I am and in others, quite probably not. But the question is purely academic as the answer can never be proved. What is important is that I am facing *my* reality. I have come to know myself, come to terms with it and know what I must do in my life. I am also prepared to accept the hurts, frustration and ostracism that I know must inevitably attend such an undertaking. *Most people form an uneasy peace with the world around them, but have little peace within themselves.* I have deep peace within myself, but will always be 'at war' with the world."

* * *

Don't use up your todays, preparing for tomorrows — they may never come.

3

LIVING WITH OTHERS

Within the 24-hours-of-all-our-days job of living with ourselves, we spend our waking hours trying to live in peaceful co-existence with others. If we are successful in achieving this complex operation on a personal level, it is a great step towards the infinitely more complex achievement of doing so at an international level. I wonder if the people who: "Can't understand why it's so difficult for countries to get along together . . ." ever pause to consider just how 'easily' they get on with their wives, families, business associates and fellow workers — and they at least speak the same language!

Ego-altruism

As may already have become apparent, I am an unashamed proponent of egoism. If I don't develop myself, how can I possibly offer developed advice to others? Development of self, for these purposes, is the basis of the doctrine of ego-altruism. Whether my egoism becomes egotistic is a moot point — beyond the undeniable fact that there isn't a human being who is not egotistic to some degree. As egotism is not only a matter of degree, but opinion, too, it is, like all opinions, unprovable in an absolute sense. Most people probably define egotism as the stage at which egoism either becomes offensive to them, threatens their own ego or possibly, shows it up by reflection. I think all three reasons are more likely to be unconscious reactions than deliberated ones.

That much of what I write will appear egotistic to some people, is inevitable. Its apparent degree will vary in proportion to the individual's ability (or desire) to understand the motivation behind it . . . and the extent of his own basic inner security. I assess my motivation as being an honest self-exposure, to allow the reader to know the true me, the better to assess the value and sincerity of my remarks. This self-exposure carries no fear of the consequences of 'society's' conventional judgement. I am content to be thought of and judged in the many ways in which different people will inevitably react to a maverick — an individualistic, untamed and free (thinking) creature!

"I've been there too"

Some passages are included to show that: "I've been there, too" and therefore can really understand and sympathize with other people's problems, fears and hopes. It is only by experiencing something personally that we have a chance of truly understanding what the other person is going through. It's amazing how many of us think that our particular problems are quite unique and have never been experienced by anyone else. But, at one time or another, we all face remarkably similar situations during our journey through life. The help and understanding we seek at such times is all around us, if more of us are prepared to be open both to asking for — and giving — that help.

Let a smile be your traveling companion and life-lubricant

A smile is a tiny investment of effort that pays handsome dividends. It leaves both giver and receiver feeling good and so oils the gears of daily living. A smile is also a unit of international currency, convertible and acceptable everywhere — and a passport that knows no frontiers and reaches all people's hearts. There can be no greater gift than the ability to make someone else smile.

Just one smile

If I can make one sad-looking person smile, I feel I have done something worth while and constructive that day. There's too little happiness and caring and too great an excess of their opposites.

* * *

Another tiny effort — to be courteous and polite — also yields high dividends. It takes only a fraction more than the nil effort of being discourteous or indifferent. The disparity in effort invested is indiscernible, but the difference in the return is immense.

Timeless magic

Driving into Bangkok, I passed a gorgeous Thai girl by the roadside: as I whipped round in my seat, her head turned too, and she peeped over her shoulder . . . That magical instant when two people's eyes meet . . . destiny may never intend them to meet again, but that's quite unimportant. That moment is a forever-moment, a moment of the beauty of sharing, and of what does life consist but moments, and what is more beautiful than to share? A smile, a wave — and a memory . . . two lives that crossed, paused — and passed on into timelessness.

Kill them with politeness

If we oppose violence, physical or verbal, with like violence, win or lose, we stand to be hurt in the ensuing conflict. A useful practice, applicable to many situations in life, is to calculate how people think we will react — and then do the opposite. It leaves an assailant floundering hopelessly, for if we meet violence with a side-step, or politeness (a potent weapon), robbed of his expected opposing force, he will often fall flat on his face — literally or metaphorically. He will also look stupid and puerile — the most apt description for all violence.

Where the hurt really is

When we understand why someone is deliberately hurting us, the knowledge greatly diminishes the hurt. In time, it can all but eliminate the hurt and replace it with a feeling of compassion for those hurting us. They are the ones who are really hurting inside.

Vendettas can backfire

When a person is motivated by vengeance, there's poison in his system. Who is likely to suffer most?

The best outlet for anger

When we're all steamed up and raring to go on the warpath against someone who has incurred our displeasure, here's a tip to come out on top. It's disastrous to act when in an emotionally charged state — a boxer who has lost his temper has lost the fight. Vent your righteous indignation and wrath on the long-suffering, available ear of your wife or girlfriend. If well versed in the art, she will interject the appropriate noises of disapproval, agreement and sympathy at the right moments (usually when you pause to draw breath in your tirade!)

Alternatively, dip your pen in vitriol, sear the paper with lacerating prose and read it out aloud — with all the requisite inflections. Then put it back in your desk — not in the envelope. The next day, when your ire is spent and the venom drawn from your system, call up the offender, or write another letter. Calmly, coldly and logically state your case, with icy politeness. *That* burns with a much hotter fire than all the heat generated by the initial, emotional reaction.

Lie-weavers' webs

It may be easier to be dishonest, than honest, at a given moment. That's the coward's way out and anyway, lies usually come home to roost, sooner or later. A lie, once initiated, must be kept up. So one is committed to weaving an ever-more complicated web of fabrication, to preserve the original lie's 'authenticity'. If several are running at the same time, it must be confusing to have to remember exactly what one has told each person. It's all too easy to become enmeshed in the intricacies of one's own web. It's usually easier, long term, to take the hard way of honesty — at the moment when one still has the choice.

In a relationship, of any duration, honesty is vital. If one lie is detected, how can one be sure again? That one deceit could be the first of many, or the most recent of a long line — how could one possibly know?

The impenetrable armor of nakedness

The greatest strength in life lies in having nothing to conceal. Our open 'defenselessness' becomes an impregnable fortress. We are immune to attack. There will still be attacks on our integrity, made out of jealousy, but having no foundation, they can be brushed aside easily.

Tit for tat

Anyone who asks blunt, direct questions, must be prepared to face the consequences of equally blunt, direct answers.

One man's *meet* is another man's put-down

Some people inflict painful hang-ups on themselves out of an insecurity, which makes them have an over-powering need to be liked by *everyone.* If someone doesn't like them, they take it as a mortifying personal put-down. They seem unable to realize that, just as everyone is different, so are likes and dislikes. It would be impossible, with the variety of human differences, for everyone to like everyone else.

However, there are plenty of people who will get on well together. So when you don't click with someone, don't continue chasing dead ends or retire from life as a failure — move on. There are other constructive, mutually beneficial relationships for you . . . around the next corner in life.

Self (ish)

Being ourselves — completely — is only being selfish if we are with someone who doesn't, or doesn't want to, understand us. In which case, there isn't much point in spending much time with them!

Multiple standards

What we expect of ourselves, in standards and behavior, we have no right to expect of others. He who persists in expecting, usually ends up disappointed and frustrated.

The ages of free speech

Both youth and age permit the luxury of total freedom of speech — to say what one wants and to mean it. Youth, unknowingly, and therefore sometimes hurtfully, says too much. It is less selfish, than ignorant. Age, implies the age when one has overcome one's inhibitions to again say what one feels — but now knowing full well its effect on the recipient. It does *not* imply the age of 'couldn't care less!'.

This freedom carries the responsibility of not deliberately hurting, by being too open, those who can't take it. The responsibility is not always recognized or implemented by all who have reached this point. Consideration and discretion sometimes trail behind in their development. In between the impetuousness of youth and the supposed wisdom of age, lies a long period when people can be afraid to say what they mean, for a multitude of reasons.

The pace of ages

Both the very old and the very young need the indulgence of our patience. Neither moves at the physical or mental pace of the in between years.

Life's power source?

Most people, one time, several times, or almost all their lives, lean on others or cry on their broad shoulders. At the end of these long lines are a few strong individuals — who have only themselves to turn to and lean on. Is that what makes them strong enough to carry the others? Or could they be tuned in to the power source of life, consciously or unconsciously understand this, and draw on it, in their time of need for replenishment?

So little could mean so much to so many

If occasionally we paused for a moment to consider how so little can give so much, there could be more happiness in everyone's life: a card, a phone call, a word, a caress — simple actions that show we thought about someone and *care.*

The people game

People are often surprised at, and even critical of, the open way I talk to strangers about myself. Someone has to open the people-communications game — which is more complex than any chess tournament — by 'exposing' himself. How else can we find a common interest, if neither side volunteers any information about himself? People are generally wary — they've been hurt and snubbed too often when they opened themselves in the past. I accept that being hurt is part of being open and therefore vulnerable. This realization reduces the possible hurt to negligible proportions and it's easy for me to open the game. It's very worth while and the contacts I have made are legion, with whom much happiness has been shared.

Friends and friendship . . .

The time it takes to get to know a person is contingent upon how open we are prepared to be with him or her — and how soon . . . and, vice versa.

* * *

If we have a 'friend' whom we do not respect, then we better 'reclassify' him under: 'acquaintances'.

* * *

A true friend is someone we can really be ourselves with — and vice versa — AND someone who, when our 'ship' is foundering, doesn't sail away, apparently afflicted by sudden deafness to our cries — the deafness of indifference.

. . . and those who need them

One of the most easily and frequently misinterpreted impressions given out (unwillingly) by people, is shyness. So often we take it for a very opposite attitude — stand-offishness — and so ignore a lonely soul, branding him accordingly. Next time you come across a 'stand-offish' person, run a double check on him. Then see if you can help him come out of himself and into life. He would give anything to be able to do that.

Loneliness

It's easy to feel alone in a city full of people, when we don't know anyone or anywhere to go. Sometimes fate is kind and arranges a meeting — suddenly, we belong. If not, we're on the outside, incommunicado, our life-line severed — especially if there are also linguistic problems.

All around are groups of happy people — or at least, looking happy — and many lonely ones, craving contact as much as we do, no one knowing how to make it. This is what drives traveling businessmen to clubs for girls (probably more for companionship than sex), for once the day's work is over, their purpose is gone and they are alone again.

Even at home, after a workday, with its feeling of purpose and belonging, many people become similarly lost and lonely. This is why some turn into such sociable extroverts, for they can never bear to be alone. However, the more we can develop ourselves to enjoy our own company, the less lost we will feel — anywhere.

Even 'swine' have pearls

The most uninteresting, boring person we meet has at least two things we may not know and can learn from him: his job and hobby, so be patient with him.

Unselfishness

More often we should try thinking about someone else instead of only ourselves; try doing something for someone else's sake and not just for money. Let the giving be the getting. The rewards can far outweigh the investment — even though some people will consider it far too idealistic.

Drilling for 'white gold' — in people

Most people are 'nice' — if we are 'nice' to them. We shouldn't be put off too easily, if they don't respond immediately. It's there in everyone — with some, we have to dig deeper to reach it. It depends on how many layers of defense system cover it — layers built up from years of being hurt or rebuffed. Oilmen have to drill deeply for the hidden, buried riches of 'black gold'.

Excavating decency

It can be rewarding to touch deeply into people and allow them to bring out into the open and express the repressed and near-forgotten feelings of 'the decent things in life'. Modern society has forced many of them under (subconscious) ground as undesirable, archaic values, subject to superficial ridicule. This attitude has eaten so deeply into some people, without their realizing it, that it has become an integral part of them and is no longer just on the surface.

Do-gooders . . .

Why is it often considered 'fashionable' to put down someone who chooses to do something good for someone else? Everyone derives pleasure and satisfaction in widely differing ways: some by acquiring power, some by amassing money, others by military conquest . . . what can be so wrong or derisive about someone who happens to find enjoyment by making others happy or by improving their lot?

. . . and their rewards

It is also not unreasonable for them to enjoy *some* recognition for whatever they have achieved, as apart from deep inner satisfaction, there is rarely any tangible, or other reward. Of course, there are some saints who do not even seek recognition, but then they really must be 'Saints'.

Giving

It *should* be easier to give and forget, than to receive and forget. Unfortunately, some givers 'remember' their 'gifts' — which makes their recipients want to forget such 'investments'.

Giving . . . is getting happiness

People who follow the pure philosophy of giving: doing something for someone for no other reason than the pleasure of giving and helping — giving and marking it down in the book as something to be returned is not true giving — these people enjoy more happiness than any others. They deserve to.

Confidences

Most of us are the recipients and supposed guardians of someone's confidences — how well do we guard what has been entrusted to us?

Shadows

People flit in and out of our lives like so many shadows. Some are longer, deeper than others; some almost solidify into permanent fixtures; others rematerialize from the past. We all flicker but briefly across the shadow-lantern of life.

Making-up — beforehand

It can be fun 'making-up' after a quarrel. However, quarrels (in friendship or marriage) usually destroy some part of the relationship, even though they're normally about some petty matter. It would be more constructive and harmonious if stubborn, stupid pride took a back seat while the 'making-up' was done — *before* the quarrel developed. Any moment is better filled constructively than destructively.

"Nothing ventured, nothing gained"

We must always be opportunists, in the sense that whatever circumstances life presents us with — even through our own errors — we should be able to recognize the opportunity and take advantage of it. Generally speaking, the worst than can happen when, for instance, we ask for something, is that the person says no — what have we lost? At other times, we just can't go wrong by having the small amount of guts necessary to 'venture'.

Self

Too often, we are so wrapped up in our own egos and /or problems, that we won't, or can't step outside ourselves sufficiently to really understand someone else and *his* problems.

"Little boxes made of ticky-tacky . . ."

Some people apply set solution formulae to what they suppose are stereotype problem situations that they or others get into. They fail to take into consideration that each person is a unique individual. His problem will have a uniqueness which requires that it be studied, on its own, and a solution tailor-made for it. That a set solution *may* fit the situation is possible, but should never be assumed.

Speak as you act . . . and act as you speak

To retain any respect we may have earned from our fellow-men, we must always make sure that our actions bear out our words . . . and vice versa.

Verbal diarrhea

"If you've nothing good to say about a person, don't say anything." For compulsive talkers, this excellent axiom can be taken a stage further: "If you've nothing worth while to say, shut up!" To spout words for the sake of breaking silence, or worse, to hear one's own voice, is a bore. Silence, in its proverbially gilded state, can be very beautiful between two understanding people.

Charitable honesty

If we do have to say something unpleasant about a person, because we've been asked for an honest opinion, that's one matter, but to run someone down for no reason, only lowers us in the listener's estimation. How does he know we won't be doing the same to him, five minutes later? Even when we have to give an unfavorable opinion, let's see if there are any *genuine,* extenuating circumstances, before totally damning a person. If he has good points, as any human must, let's remember to include them, too.

Customary dishonesty

Don't underestimate the value of being honest with people who are used to constant minor and major dishonesty — like customs officers.

In(di)gestion

At any period in life, each individual has reached a certain level of receptivity and understanding. The skilled communicator must learn to recognize this and gauge it accurately. To exceed it, is not only a waste of words, but risks destroying the value of what has already been said — through indigestion from ingestion of excessive information.

Egos: theirs and mine

I am neither impressed by, nor do I accept the valuation implied by title, rank or money — all the outward vestiges and worldly trappings of man's basic insecurity. I've mixed with both ends of the so-called social scale — from beggars and thieves to nobility and celebrities — and most of the in betweens. As a result, I regard all people as human beings, just like me, and accord them the respect they deserve — based on *my assessment* of their integrity, achievement and contribution to the world. *My* assessment, because I have to live my life by my judgements — not someone else's. I call few men "Sir"; the term implies respect. They have names, as I do, which suffice to distinguish them. My preference is always to use first names. Otherwise, "Mister" fills the requirements of courtesy.

The formality barrier

Formality usually serves only as an obstacle to full communication between people.

Great men and punks

You can assess a man's true 'bigness' by the way he treats 'little' men — people in servile or subordinate positions. The really great man, being a gentleman, will treat them with the consideration anyone deserves, no matter what his station in life. He who only affects greatness, reveals his lack of inner security (and breeding) by treating them like dirt — behavior which boomerangs to clearly depict the little punk's true character.

* * *

No one likes giving orders as much as little men — who have to take them.

Does patience herald senility?

We (adults) fret at children's fidgeting and inability to sit still when they have to wait with us. Their restless, curious spirits have no time to wait. They're at the outset of their most exciting voyage of discovery and every moment of enforced inactivity is a major tragedy. Is our own stoic acceptance a symptom of premature senility — and is patience truly such a virtue?

Authority — military or civil

"Dear Boss . . ."
Instead of considering employees as people working *for*
you, try regarding them as working *with* you. The results —
with respect maintained — can be surprisingly pleasant and
commercially successful.

* * *

It's a good idea to be capable of doing one's employees'
jobs. Until we've put ourselves through something, we can
have only the sketchiest idea of its reality. By doing so, we
can better understand their problems, try to improve their
conditions and so gain more respect and increased output
from them.

* * *

When in a position of authority, try asking, before
resorting to ordering. A "Thank you", too, goes a long way
towards having the next 'order' carried out more willingly
and efficiently.

Togetherness — with authority

An officer, leading troops into battle may be scared to
death. Although he should cheerfully admit it to his men, he
shouldn't show it. A subtle distinction, but the admission
enables the men to identify with another human being,
feeling as they do, BUT fighting it and succeeding in
controlling it. This gives them the best possible example to
follow, for one of a leader's prime responsibilities is to
inspire his men with an example which is *possible* for them
to follow. Teamwork, not lone heroics, wins battles — on
and off the battlefield.

Leadership

A composite of many attributes fused into an intangible
quality, possessed by a rare few, which others sense and
follow.

Motivated axes

Generally, when people give advice or an opinion, they have some axe to grind, some ulterior motivation — sometimes deliberate, often unconscious. The skill in listening to such advice, is to assess what is the axe or motive. Subtract that element and consider what's left, if any, of unbiased advice — unbiased in the sense of being in our interests, not theirs!

Accidents of birth

Good looks — given that they are in the eye of the proverbial beholder — are only an accident of birth (or the plastic surgeon's skill) and merit no credit to their possessor. Society has perennially smiled favorably on those so blessed by fortune, but to a ludicrously disproportionate degree. Equally stupid is the supposition that a person can have either looks *or* intelligence, but not both. Should an innocent person be so inconsiderate as to possess both, he may face irrationally prejudiced envy and rejection.

Mental illness

Here is a suggestion as to why people used to mete out such appallingly barbaric treatment to the mentally ill, and still have a certain fear of them even today. It is not a tangible, visible illness like a cold or measles – these we can understand, their obvious symptoms appertain to the physical body. Mental illness visits the intangible, invisible areas of the mind. There it may warp or waste away a portion of the brain – just as some diseases will warp or waste away a limb.

Ignorant reaction to a mentally ill person (or to anything not understood) is fear of the unknown. It often follows this pattern: first we ignore his symptoms, in the hope that they'll go away; when they don't we resort to ridicule (nervous laughter might be more apt!); finally, we attack savagely, lashing out blindly to protect ourselves – from what – an unpleasantly near reminder of our own sometime behavior?

Stop worrying

There's no point in telling people not to worry. If they follow this negative 'advice' and try not to think of whatever it is that is worrying them, they cannot help but be thinking about it. The only solution is positively to replace the worry thoughts – which are negative and non-constructive – with constructive alternatives. If something's wrong, either they should rectify it, or if that's not possible, they might just as well *do* something else. Further worry won't do anything more than waste time – theirs and ours.

However, putting worries into words and expressing them to a sympathetic listener can sometimes give the words wings, which will fly the worries away. But when you keep worries inside, eating away at you, they have leaden feet.

Proportional reduction of aggrandizement

The less important we really are (and inside we know), the more we try to inflate our importance. Not unnaturally, in proportion to how important we try to appear, people will do all they can to cut us down again, at least to our true size, if not further.

Personality vs non-personality

The stronger and more definite is one's personality, the more one must expect to polarize feelings about oneself into the extremes of love and hate, the latter often tinged with envy and jealousy. This polarization is certainly preferable to the inevitable gray wishy-washiness of trying to be all things to all men and ending up as an indefinable non-person.

Demolition

Sadly,there are more people who will tear anything good down to their lower level, rather than benefiting from the example to elevate themselves.

Few people are big enough to admire the achievement of someone better in the same field of endeavor. More are so small and petty that they do all they can to detract from the person's performance. They also run him down in other ways — behind his back — while all smarm and smiles to his face.

The age of success

When we find we have reached the stage in life when people come to *us* with business proposals, instead of the reverse, we can assume that we are finally regarded as being successful — or merely older!

4

COMPETING IN LIFE

The majority of us live in a competitive society. I have found that the lessons learned through competing in sport are often analogous to life, and vice versa. I choose to propound the lessons of fighting 'clean'. Those who wish to fight 'dirty' need no encouragement — only pity, for their emptiness.

Amateur sport

To compete in a sport, from which one does not earn one's livir.g, for the personal satisfaction of overcoming the challenge, and for the occasional honor, that, is true, amateur sport.

Leaky roofs and shaky foundations

Participating in a sport for fun is one thing. But if you are a competitor, set on reaching the top, you must be prepared to give yourself *utterly;* to 'sweat blood' and to learn to swallow the bitter pills of humiliation and still come back a winner. What of the long road to the top? How does one acquire the skill that can take one even near Olympic standards? That is the ultimate goal which deserves a place in the spirit of any ambitious amateur competitor.

Like the lowliest or grandest dwelling, skill is built one brick at a time and firmly consolidated as it progresses. The bricks are the foundation of basics which must be there to sustain you when the pressure's on. The roof is the mental approach with which you cover the bricks. There are many competitive sportsmen with leaky roofs — and shaky foundations. Those who are sound, move up steadily by sheer determination, a burning ambition to win (allied with the desire to overcome the challenge to oneself) and an unrelenting application of the basics — governed by a totally disciplined, controlled mind. The rewards — in personal satisfaction — are well worth any and all of the many sacrifices required.

Drop them in at the shallow end

A beginner at any sport must be broken in gradually and gently on something easy that he *can* do. Otherwise, he will quickly become discouraged and drop out. (It is most important to build his self-confidence and so maintain his enthusiasm.) The encouragement and confidence derived from being able to achieve the early goals will carry him, step by step, progressively higher until he either finds his level, decides it's not for him — or goes on to aim for and, hopefully, reaches the stars.

Do it naturally . . .

Generally speaking, our instincts and reflexes are far superior to our calculation and thinking procedures. If only we would trust and believe in these gifts and, in effect, 'let them do the job', we'd all do a lot better at most sports. An ideal combination for success in many sports is a relaxed body and a 'tense', keyed-up mind. But, it is absolutely vital not to let one seep into the other, or the results will be disastrous.

. . . and be natural

In any sport, the more natural you are and the more comfortable you feel and look, the better you are likely to be. However, the odds are that the expert's easy grace didn't just happen overnight, but came as the result of years of painstaking experimentation and application. That this naturalness eludes many sportsmen is often because, as with many things in life, many people have a great penchant for complicating things which only require basic simplicity.

EMOTIONS PROHIBITED: Sportsman at work!

Don't draw attention to your mistakes by a display of temper or dejection. A man who shows his emotions in this way is one who cannot control them and will inevitably make more mistakes because of it. What does showing up your mistakes achieve? It simply delights the opposition who will reasonably assume that you are cracking up!

Few competitors like to admit a mistake could have been their fault, it is so much easier and ego-salvaging to blame anything else — like equipment, the weather, someone else. Such a competitor has set a limit on his own progress. Until he adopts the philosophy that the most important nut to get properly adjusted, is the one using the equipment, he will never amount to much in the field of competitive sport.

Moon-shots

Don't aim at the moon overnight and become dejected when you don't reach it immediately — it took man quite some time to get there! Set yourself reasonable goals and build your performance or averages steadily on those firm foundation bricks. Flash-in-the-pan houses of straw quickly collapse under pressure. And when you reach the exalted heights, don't be too disgusted with a bad score — just remember how good it once looked — not so very long ago!

Inspired progress — or retrogression?

Every so often we run into someone who is better than us in a particular sport. Sadly, many of us feel diminished by the encounter. This should not be so. Whatever standard we had at the time of the meeting has in no way lessened; it is still exactly the same. To feel it is lessened is a negative reaction. A positive reaction would be to take the better person's level of achievement as an inspiration to urge us on to doing better, too. If one human can do it, why shouldn't we? This is naturally subject to physical limitations, but beware of 'copping out' by imposing limitations that do not exist — except as excuses in the mind.

Beat yourself first, then — the others

In any competitive event, it's almost always easier to be pressing than the one being pressed. If you have to set the pace as the leader, what pace do you set to keep the opposition behind? How much reserve do you hold back? For the one chasing the leader it is generally easier, for he knows what he has to beat and can pace himself and his reserve more beneficially.

This theory (and its attendant problems) is based on the supposition that a competitor sets out to beat the other competitors. This is usually the motivating force behind the competitive character.

However, if you set out 'to beat yourself' and *set your aim high enough,* when you achieve it, there will be few, if any, in the same league. Also, you will have eliminated the problem of being governed by other competitors' pacing — whether they are leading or following. You have your own pre-set plan, which is not dependent on them. Of course, if you find yourself 'up against it', you may still have to call on that impossible bit extra. But that is what most basically defines a successful competitor — someone who pulls out that bit extra under pressure, instead of folding up and fading away. Kipling put it this way in **If**:

"If you can force your heart and nerve and sinew
To serve your turn long after they are gone,
And so hold on, when there is nothing in you
Except the Will which says to them: 'Hold on!' "

Almost there . . .

The tension eases, the victor smiles, surrounded by well-wishers, while the less fortunate move quietly and sadly away from the spotlight that, for a moment, they savored and so nearly attained.

5

WOMEN AND LOVING

The ensuing passages are presented, with affection and understanding, to all women, that they might experience deeper fulfilment and happiness in their loving and love-making; and to men, with a plea to be more than aware of gentleness and consideration in their relationships with women. And remember – no one learns to be a lover overnight, but over many nights . . .

True Love:

a beautiful intangible that cannot be defined in likes and dislikes and which loves, not because of anything, but simply — because . . . or perhaps, in spite of . . . and is rarely easy. Likes and dislikes have specific reasons, love does not.

Fine love-making:

the split-second synchronization of nature's most delicate clocks and the blending of its most volatile wines.

* * *

Love-making is a time for the most *total* freedom we can possibly experience. It is no time for inhibitions and repressed desires. Ideally it is when we should *be able to be* and *be* our most basic — even primitive — selves. Perfection in love-making may well be the skilful pairing of two strange bedfellows: primitiveness — and gentleness.

* * *

It takes a great mistress to appreciate a great lover — and vice versa. The indescribably subtle and delicate skills of love-making require a shared level of understanding and awareness for their full enjoyment.

* * *

Can there be any sight more beautiful than the soft, loving eyes of a fulfilled woman? . . . This is posed as a question, only so that men will reflect and mentally review the panorama of their concept of beauty. Those who have been privileged to be recipients of this look, should have no doubt as to their answer.

Loving . . .

is feeling as close to your partner *after* making love, as before. This is quite different to using someone for the release of sexual tensions and then no longer wanting to be with them. Although this does of necessity happen, initiated by male *or* female, ideally it should only take place when both parties explicitly or implicitly accept the relationship as being exactly what it is. Otherwise, it is more considerate not to risk messing up someone's emotions for momentary relief or purely sexual enjoyment.

The love bed

If unmarried, one normally only shares a bed with someone truly loved . . . if one is not going to make love to her at that particular time.

Love's balance sheet

It's virtually impossible to truly commit oneself to love, without the risk of being hurt. Hurt is the debit side of love — but the credit side it total, utter, indescribable exhilaration.

Love's tears

A little pearl of crystal runs down your cheek, nestling into the soft lines of your face and rolls over the down on your skin. I raise your chin with my finger and the little drop of warm moisture touches it. A gentle, half-smile peeps through glistening eyes, a little sniffle and the smile broadens. What did I do to hurt you? Can you tell me? Is it real, or some imagined wrong? How could I ever wilfully hurt your gentleness? I unfold the tight little knot of your hand, remove the crushed, damp handkerchief . . . and now it's your teeth that are glistening in a shy grin.

See-through mirrors

Eyes have been described as the mirrors of the mind or soul. Surely they are better described as windows, through which, those who know how to, can see inside. Sometimes we are lucky enough to see our thoughts reflected in a woman's eyes, but that reflection is still only a glimpse of something private, which, for precious moments, is shared.

Heartaches and breaks

Love, physical or mental, or more ideally their combination, rarely begins at exactly the same moment for any two people and almost never ends at the same time — hence the heartache of one at the outset and the inevitable heartbreak for one at the end.

Femininity . . .

is an intangible quality which exists deep inside a woman and is subtly apparent from the outside. The result is a complete woman. The blatantly external female is clearly showing her concern that *her* femininity may be only skin-deep.

An advanced Linus blanket?

People who are sexually secure and confident and lead well-balanced sex lives are generally secure, confident and well-balanced in all other areas of their lives. The reverse is as drastically destructive as the former is beneficially constructive.

[*My admiration for Charles Schulz knows no bounds. His contribution to the world of 'Peanuts' (Charlie Brown, Snoopy, Woodstock, Linus and co.), rates as the greatest, simplest and most entertaining philosophy I know.*]

Dates

The routine is dinner and the movie, followed by drinks. The drinks are for weakening the female and fortifying the male. The male's aim, after the prerequisite, awkward groping in the car, is the initial 'goal' of getting the female into bed. Sometimes, especially in America, the male and female roles are reversed!

Occasionally a woman complains that a date is being made solely for the purpose of making love and that there's no 'relationship' outside that. How much 'relationship' is there sitting at a table with your mouths full of food or in a dark movie theatre, again unable to talk? All the time, one or both parties is thinking of making love anyhow!

To me, a 'relationship' implies communication — mental and physical — and to spend that same amount of time alone together, enjoying both to their unimpeded full, would seem to be a far fuller 'relationship'.

* * *

Some girls date simply as a means of getting a free meal. Some men consider that taking a girl out to dinner buys the right to go to bed with her afterwards. These two unpleasant types should meet — they could well learn a sobering lesson from each other.

'Showing off' . . .

our accomplishments to a girlfriend, or prospective wife, is so like the courtship display of male birds and animals to their prospective mates.

A love(ly) idea(l)

Many women are in love with the idea — and the ideal — of being in love. They are almost in love with love itself.

Marriage: love or loneliness?

It's a sad commentary on marriage that many people involve themselves in ultimately unhappy relationships, because they prefer boredom to loneliness.

Love — a myopic archer?

When one looks around and sees some of the mis-matched couples and sad, one-sided love affairs, one is strongly inclined to believe that love really is started by a short-sighted Cupid, firing random arrows.

"Sure, I'm happily married, but . . ."

Complaint from *a* girl — representative of countless girls:
"I only meet happily married men . . . you know, the happily
married ones who go out with other women."

The undignified chase

Women lose dignity when they chase a man. If a man
doesn't recognize and acknowledge her subtle and tacit
admission that his attentions would be welcome, then she
should realize that he isn't for her.

Take-overs and mergers

The more a woman tries to consolidate her position with a
man, the less sure he is that he wants to become a fixed
asset.

Bed — or the door?

If a woman becomes aggressive with a man, it means that
either she wants him to disappear rapidly — or that she is
very attracted to him and he isn't reacting the way she
wants, or quickly enough. It takes a certain amount of
pleasantly acquired skill (and scars!) to know the difference.

Tough cookies with soft centers

Inside every tough, hard woman is a soft, gentle one longing to come out and bask in the warmth of strong, male gentleness.

Who rules the roost?

Generally, when a woman attempts to dominate a man, she is really pushing him in the hope that he will turn round and assert his position of ultimate authority, for when a woman succeeds in taming a man, she bitterly regrets it — and despises the man who permitted her to.

WANTED: by a strong woman — a stronger man

The more intelligent and mentally strong a woman is, so will she find it proportionately harder to meet a man she can respect and with whom she can achieve her ultimate goal — that of feeling like a woman. Often, frustrated by 'calling the tune' with every man she has known, she will, in desperation, play-act the role of being the weaker, submissive female. This often results in a sadder, even more frustrated parody of a 'real woman'.

Love is blind?

Emotion, when interpreted by a woman who *wants* to be in love, will permit her to see only those sides of a man's character that she wants to see and will dismiss everything else as unimportant, or even non-existent. The world's most skilled con man could not do a better job than that which she so willingly inflicts on herself. Love may be blind, but it's often a voluntary condition.

Jealousy . . .

when linked to possessiveness between man and woman, is a reflection of the feeler's awareness of his own inadequacies. It is a lack of sufficient character and qualities to induce one to want to stay with the other of his own free will. The emotion destroys mainly the feeler, eaten out by his own sad, basic insecurity, but also adversely affects all those whose lives he touches. It succeeds principally in achieving exactly the opposite of the effect desired, by driving the other person progressively farther away. A person who deliberately tries to provoke jealousy in a loved one, to bolster up his own insecurity, is playing with a fire which will probably consume both of them. Mutual love and respect can only flourish in freedom and trust.

Changes and reflections

So often we try to change a loved one — only to dislike the usual result — a reflected image of ourselves.

Once in a lifetime

There are few greater tragedies than, when years of being disappointed, let down and deceived, have so blinded a man or woman with myopic cynicism, that they are unable or unwilling to recognize the one rare and genuine individual who may chance into their life sphere. Failure to recognize this is usually followed by hind-sight realization, emptiness and remorse. Such people don't happen along too often.

Attraction: fragile, intangible and highly perishable

Why must most relationships be temporary? They usually start with a physical attraction which can last a night, a month, a year, twenty years, but rarely for ever. Attraction is a most fragile, intangible quality and highly perishable. One is never quite certain why it is there in the first place, nor why, one day, it is equally suddenly gone, again without any precise explanation.

When a physical relationship dies, most people want to move on, even if they can't. The running-mate of physical attraction is mental attraction. Generally less sudden, less overwhelming, it is a rapport which grows and develops in time. Up to a point, the physical develops along with it, but then they part company. Why? The usual cause is that the physical attraction just fades away. But, even in those cases where it has not completely died, there is still a separation.

The ways of expressing physical love (or mental love through the physical) are legion, but they do have limits. This is especially so when compared with the limitless ability of two minds to develop a relationship. There comes a point when the mental rapport develops to greater depths than the physical.

This disparity increases as we grow older. Our physical abilities and attractiveness deteriorate, whilst our minds have almost limitless potential to develop. As the physical side of a relationship is undeniably of paramount importance, this disparity can cause breakdowns in otherwise full and fulfilling relationships.

Another inequality in any relationship is the fundamental inequality of *any two individuals.* Sometimes, one will 'vampirically' suck the other mentally dry — and so grow bored before the less 'well-stocked' of the two.

Using . . .

Even in a really close relationship, people occasionally accuse each other of 'using' one another. Is this not generally the normal, mutual give-and-take, which is so rarely exactly equal? Of course, one can destructively analyze such normal interchange down to the base motive of *purely* 'using' the other person — in which case no relationship exists any longer.

By a comparable process of irrational, destructive analysis, one could reduce sports to which people devote their professional or recreational lives, to chasing a pigskin bag filled with air around a field — or to striking various spheres covered in differing materials with an assortment of wooden or metal clubs.

When love dies, but caring lingers . . .

To have loved a person and still remain with her when your love for her has died, can be so hurtful — even when deep caring still exists. Pain is caused to the no longer loved partner, and pain is felt by the other from the guilt of knowing the pain being caused to the one no longer loved . . . but who still loves.

Physical desire

Almost reluctantly, the predominant importance of the physical side of love in most relationships must be admitted. If one no longer physically desires one's partner, it is extremely rare that any amount of caring and friendship can ever substitute for the absence of physical desire. Such feelings cannot really be pretended, for even the greatest actor would generally be seen through by the one no longer desired.

To stay . . . or not to stay . . .

A major problem facing many couples: is it better to live together with whatever is wrong in the relationship . . . or preferable to live alone, without whatever is right?

Salvaging friendship

Once a girlfriend has ceased to be a 'girlfriend', why can she not remain a friend? Sexual chemistry may come and go, but once friendship has been given, it should rarely be taken back. Parting from wives and girlfriends with anger or bitterness and remaining 'not on speaking terms', is so pointlessly negative and even destructive. All that was once there between you cannot completely have ceased to exist.

Diamonds may be a girl's best friend, but . . .

honesty and understanding between man and woman are rare and beautiful gifts of even greater value.

No formal introduction? Try this!

"Excuse me. Do I know you — or is that just wishful thinking?"

'Anticipletion!'

The next best feeling to having, is the wanting — just before the having!

Prelude to passion

In love-making, passion, by its very definition, can rarely, if ever, be gentle — but its prelude can be, and its aftermath should be. Remember, too, love-making spans the range of all emotions, from the most beautiful to the most profane.

. . . and the lion shall lie with (and be) the lamb . . .

The fulfilment of passionate love-making can reduce a man from the Herculean strength of a virile, young lion to the helpless debility of a new-born lamb — in just a matter of moments.

The secret of happiness, et al

In making love, as in making anything of any aspect of life, too many people can never imagine giving without getting — and so, life's most open 'secret of happiness' remains hidden from them — THE GIVING IS THE GETTING.

Frigidity

A woman's frigidity can generally be measured in direct proportion to her partner's selfishness or incompetence in love-making.

Love — do you make it . . . or take it?

There's a world of difference for both people concerned between love-making and love-*taking.*

A gentleman is — a gentle man

It takes inner security and gentleness to be a giver, but if a man is gentle with an insensitive woman, she may consider him queer, weak or both! The really strong man is usually the most gentle, as he feels no need to show his 'masculinity' by a boorish display of tough talk and rough actions. *The simplest definition of a gentleman is: a gentle man.*

Pub(lic) bragging Casanovas

There is only one creature who can sense a real male: a woman. Put a woman with many of the 'boys' who spend hours boasting, over interminable beers, of their sexual prowess and exploits. They wouldn't have any idea how to treat her, even if their alcohol intake had left them capable! There is truth in the saying that he who talks too much, doesn't do. Watch the silent ones, that's usually where the action is!

Attention, woman-beaters

When a man strikes a woman, it indicates he is unable to control her (and himself, too) with his mind. He has had to revert to primitive, physical violence. Even allowing for the provocation that women can give (but it's not one-sided!), there is rarely justification for the physically stronger hitting the weaker. Some creeps can't resist beating their women, to demonstrate how 'manly' they are, in asserting their 'male authority'. Some strange women enjoy being the butt-end of such moral weaklings — they've both got problems!

Basic sexual security — male and female . . .

Woman is more basically secure in her femininity than man in his masculinity. We men waste much time and effort proving and re-proving this Achilles heel of our nature. This may be something to do with having an external sex organ. It must be erect to function properly and must perform an ejaculation to satisfactorily climax love-making. Any number of subtle factors can instantly reduce it to limp uselessness, retard or prevent ejaculation. We are therefore constantly 'put on the spot', by having to prove our masculine ability — to avoid embarrassment and ridicule from a *non*-understanding female. The female, with her internal organs, is never subjected to this apparent indignity. No matter how she feels, the most she *has* to do is lie back, accept the male and perhaps give a believable semblance of achieving a climax.

. . . and alcoholic 'security'.

Some unfortunate men have to fill themselves with drinks, to muster up enough courage to go to bed with a woman. Then they often find that all the booze has rendered them physically incapable.

The male boor . . .

Super-colossal ego makes many men presume that not only should every woman be ready to leap into bed with them, but that she should consider it a privilege that they have deigned to consider devoting a few precious moments of their time for their gratification with her. They also expect their women to have perfectly conditioned bodies, while they have the audacity to waddle in and let their beer-filled bellies spill out of their trousers on to the poor woman's body — and they wouldn't consider for a moment that they could be quite repulsive to her.

. . . and its fragile ego

When a woman doesn't want to go to bed with a man — for whatever reason — some 'rejected' men will petulantly accuse her, to her face *and* behind her back, of being cold, frigid or even lesbian. Their fragile egos and conceit cannot cope with such an insult . . . although in *other* matters, they would undoubtedly consider themselves champions of the laudable principles of freedom of choice!

Equality — male and female

Male/female equality in every possible, workable way is an excellent ideal. However, for marriage or any male/female relationship, a good example can be taken from a form of corporate division of power. A shareholding of 51%-49% gives maximum possible equality, but still retains the controlling factor of one party. This 'power' does not therefore appear as a constant dominating/domineering factor — as it would with a 90%-10% division. Nevertheless, it is there to be invoked as and when required.

In any organization, from the largest to the smallest (two people in a business or personal partnership), one person must make final decisions and take ultimate responsibility — majority votes excluded. Ideally, this should always be after consultation with and consideration for the other party. In any male/female relationship, this one person should be the man. If not, the resultant reversed roles become another major factor contributing to broken marriages and relationships.

Applying this to love-making — it is the man's *duty*, above all, to be considerate, but also to be man enough to make his woman *feel* like a woman. Many men either fail to achieve this or equate it with being rough and tough — behavior guaranteed to repel most women. The subtle skill is control through firm gentleness, combined with giving instead of taking. The result is that both partners in love-making achieve complete fulfilment, because they are able to be totally their own sex. This will often make a woman become girlishly shy or feel 'like a teenager', as it strips away adult responsibilities, which often masculinize much of her life.

After being made love to in this way, the woman may then 'take the lead' — without courting the unsatisfying dangers of initial reversed role love-making. She should be 'given the lead' by the man and not take it without such an understanding. This, ideally, should be tacit rather than expressed. But it is almost always better for the first act of love-making to be in the man's control and let it be this which may arouse the woman into wanting to take the next initiative.

Fidelity — male and female

The myth that women are by nature more faithful than men, was created largely through centuries of conditioning by a male-dominated society. Firstly, man's ego, insecurity and selfishness made him feel free to do as he damn well pleased, but let *his* woman as much as look at another man . . . the so-called double standard.

Secondly, he had no wish to be father to someone else's child. In the past ages of inadequate or non-existent contraception, this was all too likely. Now modern contraception has removed woman's fear of unwanted pregnancy (and man's irresponsibility) and put her on an equal footing with man in sexual relationships outside marriage. However, this 'blessing' of equality can create for women the problem of defeminizing themselves (Women's Lib movement, *please* note!), which could turn the blessing into a tragedy.

The major difference in male and female physical make-up — the male's genital organs being external — makes him more susceptible to the desire for 'sex', pure and simple, as a relief to the often unbearable frustrations built up by having desire aroused, but unfulfilled. In some women, desire is slower to be aroused, but once aroused . . .! However, many women have desires, just as strong and frequent as men, but are constrained to having to wait for an approach by a man. That men can go out 'hunting' is accepted by male-conditioned society, but for women to do the same thing — unthinkable!

If a married man talks to a woman (or vice versa) — the socially acceptable practice of social (mental) intercourse — is he or she being unfaithful? Apparently not, but should they have sexual intercourse, they are. Which relationship can have greater depth — the physical or the mental? The answer is obvious and also its conclusion: one can commit a greater degree of 'infidelity' in mental intercourse. The mind is limitless, while the physical side, by comparison, is limited.

This is still looking at 'fidelity' conventionally and negatively. How do we grow in life? One major way is meeting people and exchanging ideas and experiences with them. So, is it a sin to wish to develop one's experience of life? OK, you say, but you don't have to go to bed to do that. Between people who share mental and physical attraction, there will usually come a limit to mental communication. They will come up against the invisible barrier of the remaining inhibitions, preserved by lack of physical contact. Where two people have shared physical contact and love, they have had the opportunity to open themselves completely to each other. Then, there will be an ease between them, in place of the previous slight tension and scarce-concealed, held-back feelings and desires. If mental attraction was there in the first place, what *more* harm (*if* it is harm) can be done by joining their bodies? Their minds are already joined . . . and what is so sacrosanct about the casing which holds the mind?

Each of us is a unique individual. There may be others like us, but no one duplicates us exactly. When two unique individuals are together, a unique third entity is created — the resultant sharing and intermingling of the two individuals. In turn, what they share together cannot be duplicated. Even assuming the ideal where each gives the other his 'all', it is an 'all' with the limitations of being that of only one individual. Everyone's personal world contains many individuals.

Given that we grow by exposing ourselves to people and experiences — mental, physical and their combination — is it not positive and constructive to allow that a person thus added to, can be a fuller person for his long-term 'mate', instead of a diminished person — as society regards the participant in a 'casual affair'? It is the insecurity in people's unity that makes them afraid of other relationships, as possible sources of losing their partners. But if they have that fear, the relationship no longer has any firm base and, sooner or later, the inevitable will or should, happen. 'Should', because if people are unsuited, it is better for both to be free and have a chance to find happiness with *a* right partner — for however long it may last. Why a time limitation? We all change and grow in life, but rarely at the same rate or time — hence the drifting apart so regularly seen in relationships.

The essence of love is that it is a limitless and unselfish quality. Is it not then reasonable to suppose that a person can love more than one other, in varying ways and degrees, with beneficial, rather than harmful effects on the recipients? Parents love more than one child and rarely with *complete* equality or for *identical* reasons. There are also communities and nations where it is normal for a man to have more than one 'legal' wife and others where a woman can have more than one 'legal' husband. So it's obvious that the mores of our society are not the only acceptable ways of regulating relationships and that there is also more than one set of ideas regarding 'fidelity'. *Surely the only true fidelity between two people is honesty?*

Stable flings and novel rests

Those who have stability in their relationships may occasionally want the 'balance' of a little excitement . . . but they certainly do not want the consequences of such 'flings' and rarely consider them in advance. On the other hand, those who want and have the excitement of constant novelty, sometimes want to 'rest' in a stable relationship. However, as this 'rest' is likely to be temporary, it's unfair to the other person, unless she either feels the same way, or goes in with her eyes well and truly open.

Analyze love . . .

How do you define the ingredients of the chemistry of love? It's one of the few remaining secret formulae belonging to Mother Nature that has defied analysis. Computer matching can only analyze likes and dislikes, acknowledged factors in compatibility, but not in love.

. . . never!

If you are fortunate enough to enjoy a good and satisfying relationship, never seek to analyze the reasons for it, just accept it — the analysis could kill it. Generally love is blind to the pinpricks of irritation caused by annoying habits and mannerisms. These become apparent when love dies and then get measured in terms of like and dislike. They also assume larger-than-reality proportions — in exact converse ratio to their being unreally minimized while the state of love still existed.

Age-defying love

When we're in love, time ceases to exist and we even seem to cheat Father Time of his due years, as we enter a state of perpetual youth.

Lover's ease . . .

The beautiful, oblivious ease of lovers together in public contrasts sharply with the awkward tension of those who aren't yet — or never will be.

. . . and pain

When a deep love affair ends, what more can you say than this: as surely as a new day follows dark night, so life, and with it, ours, will move on to new pastures. Not only have I helped others through the experience, but myself, too. After a twelve year relationship it took a particularly long, dark night before my new day dawned — and still the memory lingered on. We only 'grow up' once in life and when that period is shared, as our marriage was, no subsequent relationship, however strong, can ever be quite the same. When it happened, I felt: "I'll walk through life with permanent dry tears in my eyes." But, of course, time does heal and life goes on.

The same mistake — or perfection?

When we find ourselves continually attracted to, going out with and even marrying the same 'type' of partner, it isn't necessarily indicative of the charge often levelled at us: that we are making the same mistake again. It can be a search for perfection. We spend some time with a partner who, in many ways, attracts us and with whom we get along well — but, subject to certain exceptions. Probably because of them, we eventually part. Then, consciously or unconsciously, we again start looking for someone who will have the desirable qualities of the last person, plus whatever else we feel we want — and minus whatever we feel we can do without! We mustn't forget that the prospective partner, lined up in our sights for scrutiny, is probably examining us with the same thoughts in mind!

Two-way sharing

In any close relationship, there is a need to share misfortune — that's fine, as long as it's balanced by a desire to share the good times too.

'Essencial' sharing

In most relationships, although we may share a great deal of ourselves with our partners, we still tend to retain something private within us. Relationships which make us want to share the very essence of our innermost selves are rare. The last sentence was deliberately not prefaced with 'unfortunately', because it is their very rarity that makes them so precious and appreciated.

The man hunters

A girl prowling the streets on her own is asking for trouble, probably wants it and generally doesn't have too much trouble finding it. Two single girls, usually playing off each other, want to be 'singled out'. Those who roam in groups, for safety, almost always want to stay that way — no matter what impression they may appear to give to the contrary!

Hollywood women . . .

a lot of beautiful meat – grossly over-displayed . . . and likely to cause indigestion from any attempt to sample its inner toughness.

The deadly female of the species

Certain female insects consume the male after mating, one wonders if some humans imitate the insects – or is it vice versa?

(Women's) liberated words

First Women's Lib wanted everything containing the word 'man' to be replaced by or at least be equally accorded the terminology of 'woman'. That was fine with 'mankind' and 'womankind', but then a leading Libber had the misfortune to fall down an open manhole in the street. Somehow it didn't sound quite right, insisting that the 'womanhole cover' be replaced . . . and that's why Women's Lib now has a 'Chairperson'.

A quote from Gloria Steinem, one of the founders of the feminist movement: "Some of us are becoming the men we wanted to marry." How desperately sad . . . but it's why I now ask women I meet: "Are you a feminist . . . or feminine?"

Lost for words?

In making love, there are many feelings that lend themselves more to subtle looks and delicate actions, than to words.

International frustration

I once met a woman who had only been able to have a climax for the first time — after *ten* years of making love previously. It is desperately saddening to realize that she, who typifies countless frustrated women the world over, should have to endure, for so long, the mental and physical agonies which result from an inability to release the pent-up tensions of love-making in final orgasm. Some women undoubtedly go through life without ever knowing the fulfilment that love-making can bring. Consequently and very understandably, they have a warped and bitter attitude toward the subject. They will probably pass it on to their children, perpetuating the problems. The blame, in most cases, can be laid squarely at the feet of men, whose inconsiderate, selfish ways in love-making rarely respect their partner's needs, but only their own momentary gratification.

One-way 'communication' — self-orientated monologs

There are so many sad, problem-filled lives, people torn apart by internal torment, and so much of it is rooted in sexual problems and maladjustment. I am particularly aware of this in women, perhaps only because I have taken the time to listen to them. The old cliché is the boss telling his secretary that his wife doesn't understand him. It rarely seems to occur to most men that their wives and girlfriends might also have problems, and want to be listened to and understood. The male ego is usually too engrossed talking about itself and expecting, as a matter of course, a sympathetic female ear — without considering providing one for her.

Misandry and philogyny

From the callous way many men treat and regard women, it's not surprising there are many misandrists (opposite of misogynist) in the world. Some turn to the doubtfully satisfying substitute of lesbianism — where at least they may find gentleness and understanding — while others just withdraw into hurt, bitter emptiness and total frustration.

Apart from championship shooting, travel and philology, I am interested (as may be apparent!) in philogyny — not stamps, women! I like and respect them as people and enjoy their company. I appreciate their conversation of the intangible values and philosophies of life, for I've never been able to get as enthusiastic about car engines and football scores as many men do!

Behind my honest enjoyment of them as people, is practical reasoning: generally, in even the briefest relationship, more time is spent talking, or talking and making love, than purely making love. So I look first for intellectual stimulus. Along with her mental sexual attractiveness, this forms the intangible combination that makes you want to be together and largely determines the degree of your mutual physical enjoyment. A beautiful face and body, whilst greatly appreciated, come in second as desirable, but non-essential bonuses.

Do as you would be done by

Every man should be chased and pestered by a homosexual. He might then begin to understand what a bore his persistent attentions can sometimes be to women — who are used to being continually chased by all and sundry in trousers. Most of them wouldn't want it any other way — despite their complaints — but a little understanding might mellow the 'tactics' of some ardent woman hunters!

Homosexuals

I wondered occasionally why homosexuals had the reputation of being more promiscuous than heterosexuals. A homosexual gave me two reasons which are quite obvious, if one takes a moment to consider them. Firstly, they do not face the risk of conception that exists in heterosexual relationships. Secondly, in heterosexual society, the woman has to await the approach of the man. In homosexual life, either side can make the approach, thus doubling their possible relationships. He also explained another aspect of homosexuality: the true homosexual apparently detests *feminized* 'drag queens', because he claimed that true homosexuality is the love of another man (even though effeminate?) — and not a male parody of a female substitute.

(This observation about homosexual promiscuity was written before the onset of AIDS.)

Monogamy . . .

There are so many interesting, lovely women of endless variety of temperament, inclination, nationality, shape, size, coloring — how can anyone possibly be expected to be monogamous? He'd miss so many beautiful experiences! BUT . . . followers of this creed *must* in fairness, accept equal freedom for women.

. . . and promiscuity

Being promiscuous is when *you* think you are, not when someone else tells you. (The dictionary defines 'promiscuous sexual relations' as those 'unrestricted by marriage or cohabitation'. It defines 'promiscuous' as 'indiscriminate' — one can, of course, be discriminating in one's choice of partners.)

I close the chapter with this personally appealing thought from a commercial for a French perfume:

"In every woman's heart there is a secret place for the memory of the man she could not have: the man who conquered her heart and then left — to conquer the world."

6

HOW THE 'TWO HALVES' LIVE

Observations of human behavior and suffering around the world

"I've looked at life from both sides now ..." say the words of a popular and beautiful song. I, too, have looked at life from both sides. The 'other side' ('other half', is an absurd misnomer) is only 'popular' by its sheer magnitude, but by no stretch of any imagination could it ever be termed 'beautiful'. It is tragically ugly and incomprehensibly cruel. I record my observations painfully, so that those who have more than they need to live, may reflect on their good fortune and then do something for those who do not even have sufficient to exist on. (Some passages are extracts, from "A Smile Is My Passport", a book about some of my travels).

PRETTY THINGS

Istanbul (Topkapi museum)

I marvel at the *things* man makes for himself, the exquisite craftsmanship and endless hours of painstaking work which go into the creation of items which will outlast by centuries those who commission and execute the edifices and *objets d'art*.

And yet, what are they but pieces of pretty colored stone and metal — for which men willingly risk and violently lose their lives in attempting their forceful acquisition. Items which pathetically demonstrate the ornate lengths man goes to in order to dress up the simplest functions of living: plates, cups, knives, forks, spoons, brushes and combs made of gold and silver, encrusted with precious gems. The pretty playthings of men and women grown bored, blase and idle through riches.

Tehran

The Persian treasure vaults fill me with a mixture of fascination and admiration — and something nearing disgust and almost horror. Displayed here are the ultimate in man's ridiculous vanity and preoccupation with material things, along with evidence of the carnage he is prepared to wreak in order to possess 'pretty things'. Imagine, as in the Topkapi museum, mundane objects in daily use, which serve the basic needs of eating, sleeping, cleaning and preening: knives, forks, spoons, plates, beds, combs, hairpins, hair and toothbrushes, mirrors, even a water jug and basin — all made out of solid gold and encrusted with emeralds, diamonds, sapphires and rubies!

They are sensationally, exquisitely, staggeringly beautiful — but how about the starving, the poor and the illiterate? So like the Vatican — stuffed with millions of dollars worth of 'things' doing no one any real good, while the Catholic nations have the worst records of poverty and illiteracy in the Western world ... Still engrossed with my sarcastic reaction to such a hoard of strictly unnecessary adornment, more gold catches my eye — my gold wrist watch. Now let's be fair about this. It should be obvious to anyone that it, too, is a totally unnecessary adornment, for I could manage very well with a plain, simple, portable sundial. Well, I guess that evens up that score!

POVERTY AND SUFFERING

Delhi — and contrast

Hideously deformed beggars — poor souls — specimens of humanity that must make any man question hard the existence of 'God' — how could anyone, with any compassion, countenance such misery for his creations? Their twisted hands grope starkly upwards from scrawny, bent frames; dull eyes peer piteously from sunken sockets, reflecting their uncomprehending resignation to an existence that can only be a living hell. Vendors call and wave, but their eyes are sharp and their bodies less scrawny. Again, contrast: the children are unbelievably beautiful and their huge limpid eyes could not fail to melt any heart. Some of the older children, quite a bit older, that is, and definitely of the opposite sex, would be welcome to melt mine any day!

Bahrain

I was angered by the contrast of the excessively wealthy few growing daily richer on oil revenues and the horrific poverty which left deformed, diseased mockeries of human beings begging and rotting in the filth-ridden dirt tracks that served as streets. They told me Aden was worse — God forbid!

Cairo

As is common throughout the Middle East, faces are prematurely old. Even the children have an old look about them. Deprivation of the bare necessities of life and the consequent suffering etch their mark deeply and early — how sad!

* * *

Violent contrasts between vivid colors and smiling faces — and the ever-present reminders of poverty, disease and malnutrition, make an uneasy, yet accepted-through-necessity, blend of sumptuous pageantry and ugly squalor.

Beirut

A sad note as I leave the waterfront and head inland past the city rubbish dump. There are families 'living' in it. They erect flimsy shelters, with corrugated iron roofs weighted down with stones against the wind, and scavenge in the dump. This is human existence reduced to a horrifyingly low level.

Istanbul

Many make their slow progress through the streets, almost bent double by huge loads carried on their backs, suspended from a band around their heads — beasts of burden, no more. Now I understand why there were so many old men last night, bent low over sticks, peering up through their eye-lids to see where they were going, tired old faces eloquently mirroring the years of suffering and hardship — and the resignation to it as the inevitable way of life.

* * *

The profusion of goods for sale (in the bazaar) is overwhelming and the jewelry displays, literally dazzling — great tiers of gold wrist bangles, powerfully floodlit, make some shops appear to have walls of solid gold ... the pathos of the rags and riches contrast is so marked here. A withered old woman in rags and a shawl, bent double from her pack-horse days, passes a 'golden-walled' shop window, pauses, raises a corner of the shawl and stares for the barest moment at the gaudy trappings of a world she will never know.

* * *

A pathetically humorous aspect of poverty: throughout the city are street vendors, standing in the pouring rain selling raincoats — but too poor to wear one themselves.

Cairo — naturalness

Expressions on people's faces, in and around their tiny mud huts, run the gamut from hate, envy and resignation to the biggest, happiest smiles you can imagine. Even adults squatting at their roadside toilet, just stare back stoically, not in the least embarrassed. It's a normal part of life to them and they probably have no idea it isn't the same for us. To them it is a natural bodily function, to which no shame is attached. I'm not suggesting we follow suit, but feel there is a lesson to be learned from their naturalness, which could be applied to other aspects of life. Some things of value can be lost in the transition from the primitive to the supposedly sophisticated. The former habit is a valid loss in the interests of hygiene, but often customs of simple beauty get lost too.

Agra

I am enchanted by the dignified, graceful carriage of the women — their colorful shawls and trousers showing the mingling of Persian influence which frequently manifests itself in various aspects of Indian life. Often carrying heavy loads on their heads, the women are definitely considered as beasts of burden by their men, yet they have twice the dignity. I remember wondering why the women wore their beautiful clothes while they were working, instead of putting on some dull work clothes and saving their 'Sunday best' for later. Then I also remember thinking, sadly, for them, maybe there is no later — it's just one long round of work in the struggle to remain alive — for what?

Tehran

I'm beginning to suspect that some of the hustle and bustle is just for the sake of passing the time and is not actually productive. What makes me suspicious is that so many others just sit around all day, doing nothing, presumably waiting for death. They seem to have accepted that there isn't much point in rushing around and tiring themselves out before their time is due.

* * *

It seems that every member of the Royal family has to have his or her own vast palace to live in and a dirty great mausoleum to be dead in. One royal chick is currently having her huge coffin built and no doubt that costs plenty. Surely the money would be much better employed, putting up some more of the Shah's low-cost housing projects, to do away with a few more slums — there are plenty left. This preoccupation with the aftermath of death is one of the more ludicrous aspects of human frailty and basic insecurity. There's plenty of living to be done here and now. In any case, how can anyone possibly prepare himself for something which probably doesn't exist, for it's quite certain that, after centuries of human existence, no one has ever come back with any information about ???? after death.

* * *

On the way back, more contrast — the huge mausoleum of the present Shah's father, and the mounds of earth in a peasant graveyard. Both ruler and serf are just the same little handful of dust inside. I wonder why the ruler couldn't have been content with a small mound too, and used the money saved to get a few peasants out of the mounds of earth, called huts, they spend most of their lives in. Seems a bit rough to spend a lifetime in one mound, only to get dumped in another at the end of it all.

I sound more like a socialist, or is it a commie, every place I get to! I'm really not looking for equality for all, that would be unbearably dull – just a fraction less disparity for those who chanced to pop into this world at the rough end of the scale.

Delhi

There are many smiling faces along the way (to Agra) in spite of the impoverished conditions they live in. But I know why they're smiling — it's their ability to laugh at their own incongruities, a classic example of which we just passed: the stretch of road running alongside the ultra-modern Central Road Research Institute was absolutely the worst bit we've covered in all our miles of travel. Same old principle as the cobbler's shoes, I suppose!

By contrast, naturally, there are also those who, like their counterparts in Egypt and Persia, just sit and wait for the end of the day — really, for the end of all their days, for they can't be looking forward to the next. Some continue to exist perhaps because they actually cherish a dream of a better tomorrow; others because they can't face the harsh alternative of ending the endless misery themselves. What is probably the vast majority, continue simply because they are caught up in the perpetual motion of existence and their thoughts have never stepped outside its narrow confines to question it.

TRADITIONS

Osaka

It's a bit unkind, mocking local customs, but I just can't help laughing at those Japanese women who are wearing western shoes, but still cling to the half-running, mincing little pigeon-toed steps they have to use to keep their ridiculous (to me) sandals on. I say ridiculous, because I view any tradition in the cold light of logic — as applied here and now. If a given custom has a practical, logical reason for continuing its existence, well and good. If, on the other hand, like many traditions, they are retained for the sake of tradition alone, there is little justification for them. Traditions often serve as unconscious security blankets for many people.

GENETICS

Taipei (Formosa)

Just as many Orientals and Blacks tend to look alike through Caucasian eyes, so they say the same about us. Their statement is untenable. Caucasians have at least four basic eye and hair colors, with endless variations of hair shading, styling and length, along with combinations of different eye and hair colors. With very few exceptions, Orientals and Blacks have brown eyes, black hair and most even have the same genetic or national hair 'style'. More than sufficient reasons to negate their retort to Caucasian remarks, which is probably provoked, quite understandably, out of hurt feelings. One must sympathize, for with the Oriental's and Black's lack of variety, Caucasians got the better end of the genetic deal.

Blacks . . . and Blacks

While living in the States, I became aware that there are almost two distinct 'types' of Blacks. There are those like my mailman, Jim, whom I simply thought of as a great guy — that he happened to have a different skin pigmentation to mine, seemed so totally irrelevant as to be unworthy of even passing consideration. Then, there are others who, when you meet them, give the impression that they are saying, in effect: "I'm black, man. Want to make something of it?"

AMERICA

Contrasts and paradoxes

America has the greatest potential for true greatness in the world. Instead of always realizing this potential, it tends to prostitute itself to the single-minded pursuit of money, relegating all other values and considerations to second place. Such retrogression of human standards is sickening and very saddening. The world once looked admiringly at America. Now attitudes are tinged with pity for a country where too many of its people are destroying themselves and their environment.

I was born Anglo-American and as a youngster was proud of both countries. As Britain continued on its apathetic and union-directed course down the drain and towards pseudo-Labour Communism, I returned to live in the States in the late sixties. I found a land of vastly separated, extreme contrasts and paradoxes. I met and formed deep and lasting friendships with some of the finest individuals I've ever encountered, but . . . I also found a most disturbing way of life, largely amoral and frequently grossly immoral — child pornography being one of the more revolting aspects. It is hard to avoid the usual clichés of the world's most advanced society, permeated by corruption and organized crime on a scale virtually unknown elsewhere.

Apart from the manic, ethic-less scramble for money and material status, I found a society dedicated to eliminating the need to think for, do anything for or entertain itself. I saw people, materialistically ultra-conformist, but ideologically and morally splintered; lost creatures desperately groping — with the aid of their analysts — through their confused values for . . . they knew not what.

Whilst I would have to plead guilty to being damningly critical in the ensuing passages, with little positive balance, I feel the proud values which epitomized the founding of America are only being kept barely alive by a relatively few fine individuals, who are struggling to keep their heads above the all-pervading morass of compromised values. One hopeful sign for the future is that one can detect a stirring among the younger generation to recapture those original 'founding fathers' values ... if they do not find themselves inexorably sucked into the credit-consumer society with a family, two cars and a mortgage to support. It is also encouraging to note that some genuine conservation, in every sense of the term, is fashionably dislodging the previously widespread profligate life-style. Even the total consumption syndrome is losing a little ground to the re-discovered, ancient virtues of being actively involved in life as a participant.

Los Angeles: cash and credit

In a huge department store, a saleswoman looks at me suspiciously when I innocently try to pay for a purchase with cash. A girlfriend explains that cash has become virtually extinct in L.A. and instead of carrying a dozen slim notes in your wallet, you now have to carry two dozen bulky, plastic credit cards. Of such absurdities is progress composed!

Hollywood Boulevard — people pageant

A fantastic variety of people: unbelievable physical beauty and outward sophistication on the one hand and on the other, the most hideously grotesque creatures going under the name of human beings that I have seen anywhere in the world — the latter mostly through alcoholic, drugged or over-indulgent deterioration, or from just plain being slobs, with their easy way of life.

Hollywood: fantasies

Some poor souls display their hang-ups and fantasies so obviously: like the balding, paunchy, middle-aged clerk who leaves his daily drudgery to dress up at night in leather jacket, tight jeans and peaked cap. He fondly imagines himself one of the diabolical Hell's Angels — but looks more like a naughty, milquetoast cherub!

Perverted heritage

The liberty and democracy the world's oppressed came to America to seek, have been twisted into license and perverted by those who can use them to further their own evil ends. Those fine words have become a mockery and a travesty of themselves. The sickness is largely perpetrated by the extreme elements of those who left other countries, fleeing from religious or criminal persecution. Where else are there more highly organized criminals or more extreme religious fanatics?

Breeding — intangible and tangible

It is generally true that people who feel the need to buy the trappings of social standing, prestige, class, breeding — neither have these intangible qualities, nor ever will. They are not commodities that can be bought, but can be acquired only through the experiences to which one is subjected, or subjects oneself to, during a lifetime. More usually, they result from generations of such exposure. This makes it difficult for many moneyed Americans who so desperately desire them and only manage to display a purchased and derisible parody of them.

Even top-class, prize-winning rabbits are not bred overnight — and they reproduce generations fast enough! However, judging from the size of many American families, one would think they are doing their best to copy the rabbits and so condense time and generations!

(U.S. population growth already exceeds that of India. By 1980, Americans should number about 9½% of the world's population. They will be consuming some 83% of all the raw materials and resources produced by the whole world. Rabbits, too, have voracious appetites).

'Class' — U.S.A.

A good-looking woman is window-shopping in the jewelry section of New York's fashionable Madison Avenue. Under her full-length mink coat, she wears tattered blue jeans and high-heeled shoes. Her mouth opens and shuts rhythmically as she masticates her oral substitute — chewing gum. At least her hair isn't in curlers — that's almost exclusively the domain of her Los Angeles counterpart.

Miami . . .

where I met every kind of person, from the ugly rich to the beautiful poor and from unlovely paupers to the well-bred wealthy.

The 'World's' best nuts . . .

Many Americans immodestly advertise their products as the 'World's best'. This unrealistic attitude pervades all levels of merchandising and even a roast-chestnut seller on New York's 5th Avenue solemnly assured me *his* nuts were the world's best! At any level, this naive chauvinism is more amusing than annoying. It accurately reflects the thinking of many Americans. They equate 'America' and 'world' and are only dimly aware (and then largely uninterested) that anything else exists outside their large continent. For some, the self-prescribed frontiers are narrower still: their state or home town.

In spite of America's size, this attitude puzzles foreigners, for America is a nation of immigrants from most of the world. The motivating factor is probably based in the sad desire of many immigrants to forget their origins and become instant All-Americans. This is partly exemplified by the shame felt by some first generation Americans for their parents' 'foreign' accents. We're all 'foreigners' . . . to other 'nationals'.

. . . and the 'World's' Tobacco Spitting Record

Less amusing are the 'World Championships' run by Americans in many sports and pseudo-sports (ie: tobacco spitting!). 'World records' (in more serious international sports!) are then claimed — despite the absence of participants from any other nation. A more modest (and honest) sense of proportion would be more likely to bring America friends, instead of righteous indignation at such flagrant and arrogant abuses.

Healthy TV = sick viewers!

After watching one night of American TV commercials, any foreigner must come to the unavoidable conclusion that Americans have the worst problems of any nation in matters of: body odor; bad breath; stomach disorders; hemorrhoids; nasal blockages; headaches (including several special varieties generally unknown elsewhere!); blood and vitamin deficiencies . . . all leading to emotional instability and general irritation; inability to cope with the day's cares without non-prescription tranquilizers — and rounded off by inescapable insomnia!

It's probably all true — but did anyone ever stop to think that most of the problems were probably induced by the repetitive series of TV and radio commercials which condition people into the states of health that necessitate the advertised medication? Thus, big (subliminal) brother advertising serves its purpose: to sell more — regardless of the cost (material or metaphorical) to the consumer. Consumer — that's a word used by advertisers and businessmen to describe a creature once known as *homo* — supposedly — *sapiens!* (Possibly *'homo sap'* would be more appropriate).

To fully understand the above, one has to realize that most ignorant foreigners labor under the delusion that it is the rest of the world that has health problems!

Isolated sexualescence

In so many ways, American parents expect their adolescent children to behave like adults socially and bear full adult responsibilities — in every way, that is, except sexually. It simply isn't possible to isolate one facet of human nature, especially one so volatile and intriguing, and conveniently put it into cold storage until an arbitrary age of adulthood is reached.

'Adulthood'?!

The following report, from their New York correspondent, appeared in England's highly respected *The Daily Telegraph:* "A boy of 5 in Memphis, Tennessee, was treated last month for gonorrhea. Investigation showed he had contracted it in relations with a girl aged 9. The girl refused to name her other sexual partners and the case was closed."

. . . and sub-juvenile sadism

"In Washington, D.C., a six-year-old boy siphoned gasoline out of a car and poured it over a sleeping neighbor. Then he struck a match and watched the man go up in flames."

(Time magazine)

The soiled sexual buck

Everywhere there is a crude emphasis on sex and a deliberate use of it as an integral part of most consumer selling. For commercial success today, read: 'commercial sucsex'. Sex has become little more than a marketable commodity. Through the mail and in sordid 'adult' (retarded) shops and movie theatres catering to an all-time low in pornography, sex is merchandised to very sick parodies of people. Even the 'legitimate' theatre and 'quality' movies cash in on this sickness. It is all the greatest put-down to what should be one of the most beautiful facets of life. God help the impressionable youngsters growing up amidst this perverted filth. For their sake, let's take sex off the market and put love-making back in bed.

Psychoanalysis — an extravagant crutch

The crutch of psychoanalysis is used so regularly, that it warrants about as little thought as that given to the weekly budget for washing powder. Why don't more people try to sort our their own problems sometimes, instead of *always* relying on someone else to do it for them? Is it just another symptom of a society which is used to having almost every labor- and thought-saving device remove the necessity of doing anything for itself? In much of the rest of the world, where average people haven't the money to indulge in the extravagance of psychoanalysis, they manage to sort out their day-to-day problems by themselves — and live comparatively peaceful lives.

SOCIETY'S DROP-OUTS
(who are not limited to America)

Perennial rebellion and its youthful losers

Each generation of youth rebels against something — generally the established order of things. It is perennially youth's temperament to do so. Today's drop-outs are rebelling against the old stand-by of any rebel: authority (in any form); America's exaggerated attention to personal hygiene and its predeliction for worshipping overdrawn male and female sex symbols.

Regarding authority, they resent any form of control and go to the self-injurious extreme of total license — especially in the area of drugs. They expect financial support and acceptance from the society they reject. If they so disapprove of society as it now exists and are prepared to contribute nothing to it, that is exactly what they should get in return — nothing. They should get out of town and join the more desirable and honest 'drop-outs' who have set up communities outside the jurisdiction of society and who work productively to support themselves.

They rebel against the cult of super-cleanliness, as forced down their throats from endless sickening TV commercials, overstressing body odor and bad breath.

They rebel against the images, created by the cinema and TV commercials, of the All-American, clean-cut, crew-cut, athletic kid next door — and his mis-matched counterpart, the big-boobed, long-haired blonde bombshell, whose sparse clothing reveals as much as possible of her sexual attributes. So, the drop-outs counter, by creating an outwardly neutral sex, where it is virtually impossible to distinguish one from the other.

As a final retort to society as they see it, they create and worship a cult of ugliness and filth, and go to considerable pains to make themselves look as repellent as possible.

In most of youth's historical revolts, the 'rebels' either gained some advance, imagined or real, or at least tried to do so. These poor creatures seem to be losers on all counts: by dropping out of society, they condemn themselves to living in conditions which border on the worst side of primitive; by abandoning cleanliness they open themselves to minor and major disease — apart from the discomfort and foul smells they have to live with; by negating the sexual difference between man and woman they lose the most beautiful aspect of creation — that such a difference exists. Finally, by defying authority to the extent they do with their excessive use of drugs, they not only sentence themselves to permanently disabled lives, but their children, too. This is not only crass stupidity, but a gross selfishness and irresponsibility to their future offspring — poor innocent little bastards!

The blank generation

Punk rock is a recent and brutal addition to the world of freaks, who adorn themselves with greased, shaven, multi-colored hair and outrageous, kinky, junk attire. Self-admitted nihilistic drop-outs and rebels who protest in despairing anger against all aspects of existing society, one must at least grant them grudging admiration for their aptly chosen self-descriptive term: 'punk'.

America's undermining affluence

A factor which makes a significant contribution to America's problems, is the excessive affluence (compared to other countries) of so many of its citizens. In recent years, it has not suffered, as has much of the world, from the destruction wrought in *its own homes and lands* by two wars. It's a society which regards many factors of life as taken-for-granted essentials — factors elsewhere considered rarely glimpsed luxuries. America, whose recent forefathers worked so hard and suffered so much to build a great nation, now has a soft under-belly of affluence-induced complacence.

This complacence is being rudely shattered in a number of very ugly ways as some of the long-concealed ills break through the surface of indifference into the harsh light of public exposure. They demand attention and bring people face-to-face with realities they have either never thought about or assumed never existed, such as: pollution; exhaustion and destruction of environment, natural resources and wildlife; food containing insecticides, possibly hazardous additives and insufficient nutrition; irresponsible overpopulation. All but the last can be blamed squarely on one factor: dollar lust.

These disastrous and rapidly worsening problems, must be recognized as unpleasant truths which daily are destroying a world that has been viewed through too deeply rose-colored spectacles.

GENERALIZED OBSERVATIONS

Rationalized larceny

Waiting to disembark from a plane in the Fiji Isles, I commented to a stewardess about a passenger, who quite obviously had an airline blanket stuffed inside his coat. She assured me it was a common occurrence. The casual indifference with which people steal from airlines, hotels, and even items of stationery from their offices, has always amazed me. They almost regard it as their 'right' and sometimes become quite indignant when challenged. But call a spade a spade, stealing is stealing . . . I can even remember 'amazing' myself!

'Simpatico'

To the Latin and romance 'races', in Europe as well as here (Mexico), the word *simpatico* has great importance. In English, sadly, we have neither a truly apt word for it, nor a corresponding feeling for its significance. Our ghastly, abused word 'nice' is as near as we can get. In essence, if you are referred to as being 'simpatico' — the world is yours and they cannot do enough for you. If you are not, you might as well go home, for it's extremely unlikely that you will enjoy any Latin country.

* * *

In the warm romance countries, people give you their hearts — because they have hearts to give and instinctively know that life's richest rewards stem from the unselfishness of this simple act.

Agricultural time

Sitting on a hillside one day with one of my brothers, overlooking his farm in Tasmania (Australia), I was struck by his reference to "next year", rather than "tomorrow" — a typically agricultural attitude to the passage of time.

Happy gamblers in Macao
(A Portugese spot on China's bottom!)

Walking round the casino, maybe I've found something I long ago had decided didn't exist — a happy gambler. Although not a gambler, I've watched big gamblers — twenty thousand dollars on the turn of a card — in London, Paris, Monte Carlo, Las Vegas, Lisbon, Ostend, Beirut and on luxury cruise ships . . . Win or lose, never a flicker of a smile, a more miserable bunch of characters I have rarely had the misfortune to observe. So much for the happiness brought about by having so much money, they can afford to throw it away for absolutely nothing. Here, everyone is enjoying himself; win or lose, the Chinese croupiers and players are joking and laughing together; it's great. If one does suffer from this particular sickness, here's the way to extract some pleasure from it.

Mexican security?

On board a plane in Mexico City almost everyone is wearing sunglasses. I wonder how many are for protection from the sun — and how many for protection from recognition? I'm always highly suspicious of those who wear dark glasses in dark nightclubs — what have they got to hide, or is it just affectation?

India: the blind ferocity of nationalism

Listening to the guide describing the history of Agra's Pink Fort, my blood begins to boil. Is there no act too foul for man to stoop to, when he wants power, sovereignty, land, jewels or a woman? The answer is an emphatic NO. Men, and women, throughout the history of the world — and especially those of the supposedly educated ruling classes, who should be the example-setters — have not hesitated to kill, imprison and torture their mothers, fathers, sons, daughters, sisters and brothers to obtain one or more of the above.

To blow off steam, I deliberately taunt the guide about some of his historical 'facts'. Each country, whose histories are interwoven with violence, have written the history books with sufficient self-bias and bending of the truth to save face. I don't profess to know whose version, if either, is correct — but it can be an awesome and sobering experience to provoke the blind ferocity of nationalism. Isn't that what Hitler and a lot of his equally unsavory predecessors around the globe have long exploited, to satisfy their own greed and the inadequacies of their inflated little egos?

Immigrant isolation in Australia . . .

Suddenly, instinct tells me that the girl sitting opposite me in Darwin Airport needs help. A ground hostess comes up and tries three languages — a sad, worried half-smile and shaken head. I try: "Sind Sie Deutsch?" and sunny smiles break through the cloudy barrier of linguistic isolation — she's a newly arrived immigrant. Friends are coming to meet her, but until then, without a word of English, she's pretty lost. It's a lonely feeling and even with my small collection of languages, I've experienced the same total isolation from people within touching distance.

. . . and intra-national communication in Istanbul!

Just before leaving the Santa Sofia Mosque, a small black kitten wanders over to make friends. No language barriers here, she purrs just like any cat!

"So God created man in His own image . . ."

7

AND MAN CREATED GOD IN HIS OWN IMAGE

As will be apparent, I am neither a follower of, nor a
believer in any organized religion. The nearest to my way of
thinking is the Baha'i religious system, which was founded
in the mid-19th century. It is based on the idea that all
religious sects are related to a single truth, that they arise
from time to time to meet the needs of evolution and that
divine revelation never ceases and will lead to world
unification.

However, my personal 'religious' beliefs are that the
distilled essence of all religions is (or should be!) very
simply: the existence of a power greater than man —
unproven, but a mental need in most people. More
practically: to aim to do a maximum of conscious good and
a minimum of conscious evil in our allotted life span.

With these simple beliefs we can cut out all religious
mumbo-jumbo, humbug and spectacle — but, we have to
make up our own minds as to the relative right or wrong of

any action we contemplate. However, it is only by taking that very responsibility that we stand a chance of growing up into mature, responsible individuals, owned by ourselves and true to ourselves, instead of always being puppets, whose moral strings are forever manipulated by others.

It is one of my aims in life to debunk whatever illogical humbug I come across. In this case, it is humbug created by some religious bodies to perpetuate their own existence, by enslaving, through fear, the minds of their followers to meaningless superstitions and rituals. Often, the 'holy ones' simultaneously fleece them of their money and goods, for the material self-aggrandizement of the religious organization.

I believe it would be extremely hard to challenge the practical simplicity and truthfulness of the essence of religion, as set out in the second paragraph. Furthermore, if you reduce ('distil') almost all existing religions to their original, uncorrupted, basic concepts, that is what they would equate to.

So, after much thought, I decided to publish the following passages, based on my observations of organized religions around the world. Although I am well aware that the way I have treated them will be offensive to some, I have done so deliberately. Hopefully, it may awaken, from a state of unconscious, accepting-without-question conditioning, those people who are prepared to take a long, hard look at themselves and their religious dogma. They may then decide that it is so ridden with illogical, old-world superstitions and today's rampant materialism, that my simple precepts make more sense for a practical dedication of their lives towards 'good' and away from 'evil'.

"Whether or not one accepts the biblical teaching that men and women are made in God's image, argues the author (former Roman Catholic nun and teacher Karen Armstrong) of *A History of God* (Knopf), it is clear the deity is a product of humankind's creative imagination."

Time, September 27, 1993

God — and his 'servants'

Some religions preach that God is forgiving — maybe he is, but haven't you met priests who proclaim this creed, yet who are nowhere near as benevolent?

Religious beliefs —

malleable self-delusions, conveniently self-adjustable.

Religions and their 'instruments'

Religions are one thing and some of them aren't too bad. Religious leaders and their underlings are quite another matter — and some of *them* aren't too good!

Religion and politics

The less said about this unseemly combination, the better. Unfortunately this view is not shared by far too many church-men.

Observations of religion made while traveling

The blood-stained lunacy of religious fervor

God, whoever or whatever you are, *if* you are, I cannot believe you could ever have intended that each race's individual ideas of you, should so often prevent their normal social intercourse and also be the cause of many of the worst killings, torturings and wars this uneasy, divided world has known. All are dedicated to the glory of the different names each group uses to describe you. Either man has made an almighty mess of your intentions — in which case, why did you let him? Or . . . there never were any intentions . . . nor any you.

Religious protocol

Much of the protocol of most religions seems to have been created by insecure, snobbish little men— often those who most loudly decry racial segregation. According to most organized religions, in their version of God's eyes, all men are supposed to have equal rights. In some Eastern religions, the separation between people arbitrarily designated — by the 'little men' — as being *different* is incredible. Certain areas are reserved for some and forbidden to others — baptized or non-baptized — women are confined to cubicles and a host of other petty segregations.

Even some Western religions make a ridiculous distinction between men and women, by requiring women to cover their heads. What possible difference can this meaningless external disparity make? Only the thoughts *inside* the head matter. To be facetious — and why not, in the face of such nonsense if God appreciates beauty, surely he would rather look down on 'Eve's' crowning glory than a collection of bald heads!

Not facetiously, but utterly incredibly . . . Muslim fundamentalists are now murdering young women, teenage students, for the 'crime' of being in a street with their heads uncovered. How can anyone believe that his version of a god could possibly condone such outrageously inhuman and ungodlike atrocities?

"The narrative Gospels have no claim as historical accounts. The Gospels are imaginative creations."

Burton Mack, *The Lost Gospel* (Harper)

The Five Gospels (Macmillan), a book produced by 74 biblical scholars who belong to the Jesus Seminar, concludes that precisely 82% of Jesus' words are inauthentic.

These two quotations were published in *Time*, January 10, 1994

If there's a God . . . it's an everywhere God

One cannot help but wonder what God — whoever or whatever that is, Allah, Buddha, call him what you will, each group creating an image and a name to suit itself — can be thinking of the ways men have chosen to interpret his principles: often merely to perpetuate and justify their own weaknesses and fears. Their pathetic, illogical belief that one structure of bricks and mortar, when called a temple, church, mosque or synagogue, is actually different to other structures built with similar materials.

If there's a God, it's an everywhere God and no place on this little planet earth is any holier than another. Jesus seemed to agree when he commented: "When two or three are gathered together in my name . . ." I believe it's even more individual — a communication between each individual and his concept of whatever God-figure satisfies his personal needs.

Even with organized religion, it's not that one is right and another wrong — rarely even in degree. Know it or not, like it or not, they mostly serve the same purpose: man's need to create an entity more powerful than himself, to whom he can turn in times of trouble and say: "Help me!". But how rarely do the same people bother to say "Thank you!", when things are going well — a basic, hypocritical defect of many. The nearer many people get to their final 'day of atonement', the more religious they — belatedly — become.

If there's a God . . . earth was formed some $4^1/_2$ **billion** (not million) years ago; the earliest humans came into existence about 2 to 3 million years ago, with thinking man a mere three or four hundred thousand years back. If God created earth, can it be even remotely conceivable, given the wildest leaps of imagination and/or faith, that this creator hung around nearly $4^1/_2$ billion years, waiting to create homo sapiens, the only creature capable of recognizing it's existence? It is certainly far more likely that, when man became able to think, he created gods or a God to meet his needs and explain his existence.

Here are three words pertaining to organized religion, two are applicable, one isn't: faith, belief . . . proof.

The back-to-front-collar set

In Burma, Bhuddist monks and nuns carry red or orange umbrellas — mere *ordinary* people are not *allowed* to carry these colors. Just how childish can organized religion become?

No other profession has such an obsession for wearing uniforms, some properly simple, but others gaudy, ornate and expensive. The sheer vanity, worldliness and inherent desire to show-off is something to be marveled at, in a calling supposedly dedicated to the non-material values of life. Soldiers legitimately wear uniforms to distinguish themselves from the enemy and avoid killing their own side. Police require them for the maintenance of law and order and in emergencies. The only emergencies priests have to deal with are the very occasional last rites at an accident, or hospital visiting — surely a simple I.D. card would suffice? What other essential or pragmatic purpose can a uniform possibly serve, in or out of church?

There appears to be an element in the religious profession of those who need to go around, saying in effect: "Look at me! I'm more religious than you (and therefore assumed to be better and superior), and to prove it, I wear my collar back-to-front." Naturally, there are many national variations of back-to-front collars. Then there are also those who have cultivated what they consider to be the 'pious' (holier-than-thou) voice . . .

Surely the truly religious person should be content with all the inner peace, serenity, security and self-assurance that we are told come from genuine faith? What lies behind their need to broadcast its hollow imitation to their fellow-men in such a pathetic and obvious way? Perhaps the answer is what differentiates between those in a religious *calling* and those in a religious *profession?* Yet, there are some Jews, who are neither professional, nor called, who still go round in public wearing the yarmulke skull cap. However, it is encouraging to note that a growing number of modern-thinking priests do have the simple humility to dress like the rest of us mere mortals.

God's 'agents'?

Organized religion could be described as a profession for people who claim to act as 'agents' or 'middlemen' with direct access to 'God' — thus implying that the rest of us do not have that privileged access. However, the universal acceptance of Christ's observation that: "When two or three are gathered together in my name ..." could cause widespread redundancy among the clergy.

Religious cocktails and Catholic celibacy

A Moslem can't touch a woman before praying, or he's considered dirty and has to wash again. No one could tell me how long before praying it was acceptable to touch a 'contaminated' female. It's all right to touch a man though!

Even stranger, Moslem priests can have two wives — they must wash a lot. I wonder how it goes? Alternating days, or three days with each wife and on the seventh day ye shall rest? Sorry, wrong religion. I keep mixing religious cocktails — come to think of it, *integrated religion* isn't a bad idea — what about one called 'Brand X'?!

How about it Catholicism, if their brand allows them two wives, doesn't it seem reasonable for your 'shepherds' to have just one? Anyway, who gave your leader what he considers to be a divine right to tell men what they should and shouldn't do with the most personal part of their private lives? You can't answer: "God", for you claim that God created man and if so, he created him to reproduce, not to be celibate.

The chosen . . . and the unchosen

For centuries the Jewish peoples have referred to themselves as the 'Jewish race' and proclaimed that they are the 'chosen people'. This carries the clear implication that everyone else is 'unchosen'. Seems like a pretty arrogant form of religious . . . and racial discrimination.

"Holy noodles!"

Shintoism is one of Japan's main religions. It seems like a step in the right direction in that Shintoism concerns itself with life in this world, whereas Buddhism worries about preparing for the unproven possibility of life in the next. That hopeful thought doesn't last long. At New Year, Shinto followers ring the bells 108 times to drive away the 108 evils and *eat noodles* — because noodles are long and so signify long life to them. Supposedly otherwise intelligent, educated, worldly, experienced adults actually believe this.

The worldly, materialistic hang-ups of religion

On learning that there were 527 mosques in Istanbul, I felt a moment of anger experienced many times before in my travels and destined to be felt often again. If some of the money devoted to these ornate, costly edifices were channeled into education and welfare programs for the desperately poor and starving in so many countries, religion would be serving a far better purpose.

It's the same every time I pass the Vatican, my anger rises, for the countless wealth it contains in material treasures is an everlasting condemnation of Catholicism and other religions which place so much value on material goods.

True religion, as taught by history's great holy men, is an almost total rejection of all wordly wealth in favor of the spiritual values of mental self-improvement and positive actions to help others. Those religions whose leaders and officials place most importance on the acquisition of money, jewelry and property, are those whose followers remain in the most extreme conditions of under-nourishment, poverty, illiteracy and ill-health.

By refusing to allow *desperately needed* modern birth control methods, Catholicism contributes greatly to the perpetuation of these deplorable conditions. People are now over-breeding to the point of their eventual self-destruction. So this becomes an especially outrageous religious idio*t*syncrasy, because it isn't disastrous only to Catholics, but to the whole world . . . strict Judaism *only* forbids *male* contraceptive methods!

Pedestrian piety?

As long as you have bare feet, you have carte blanche to do what you want in Rangoon's Shwedagon Pagoda — laugh, play, sell, love, read, sleep, eat, drink. The only reverence required is that one bares what is probably the most unattractive and dirtiest part of the human body. The imagination boggles in an attempt to fathom the reasoning behind this extraordinary ruling. It's all the more extraordinary in view of their preoccupation with elevating everything to the *highest* point for Buddha. Seems to me they're starting with the wrong end of *homo* — supposedly — *sapiens*, wouldn't it make more sense to at least try to start with 'bare' pure, clean minds?

Christmas spirit — all year round? Why not?

In the month of Ramadan, everyone (of the Moslem faith) goes round being more religious than in the other months of the year. Reminds me of Christmas when all of a sudden most people are 'nice' to everyone else. If they can muster up that much 'niceness' then, why can't they be a little more charitable to their fellow-men the rest of the year?

Kosher pigs and Hindu cows

Beyond this self-descriptive title, there is little to be added to the ludicrous and outdated superstitions, which prohibit their consumption as food. I lump them together — even though their specific origins may differ — to give a comparative view of the inter-denominational similarity of religious idiotsyncrasies.

Orthodox hypocrisy

Those of the Orthodox Jewish faith are not allowed (among many things) to drive a car on the Sabbath. In the vicinity of many synagogues, it is a common sight to see some of the faithful surreptitiously parking their cars a short distance from the place of worship. The faithful then make their sanctimonious way — on their prescribed feet — the remaining few steps.

On the Sabbath day, they're not even *allowed* to lift a finger to turn the light on. In their minds, that equates with the centuries-old enjoinder that "thou shalt not *work* on the Sabbath". (The italics are mine).

Their interpretation that the ban on *work* (specifically: 'kindling light') corresponds with a mundane necessity like turning on a light switch, is more evidence of distorted perpetuation of the past, by religious fanatics of today. What was probably once a perfectly reasonable old-world method of guarding against their version of today's executive ulcer, has now been retrogressively updated into what I call a 'religious idio*t*syncrasy'.

Another disturbing example of modern misinterpretation of ancient laws, is a ruling made by a local religious court in an ultra-Orthodox quarter of Jerusalem. The Rabbis excommunicated a man for the sin of possessing "a defiling and disgusting object" — a television set. The court considered that TV came under the general condemnation of one of the Ten Commandments, forbidding the making of graven images. (Considering the quality of some TV programs, their interpretation of 'graven images' is perhaps understandable!)

It is saddening to think how many other religious repressions and intrusions into personal liberty are furtively hidden away from the cleansing light of logic and common sense.

The tragedies of fanaticism-fueled religious idiosyncrasies

The Orthodox Jews can't even answer the telephone on the Sabbath. Imagine how you'd feel if your wife, (husband or child) were in an accident (walking to the synagogue in another town) and was dying. Because you weren't allowed to answer the phone (no one can tell you it's a permitted emergency if you can't even pick it up), you were therefore unable to be with your loved one in her last hours. An extreme, but perfectly feasible example, which brings us to . . .

The 'Peculiar People'

Some religious sects prefer to sacrifice members of their families, rather than permit blood transfusions. They start with a good philosophy: that sick minds cause sick bodies; so it's up to the mind (and their version of God) alone to heal any physical ailment. In many cases, their theory is well-founded, but, as with many religious bodies, they become blinkered to sanity by narrow-minded fanaticism. No amount of healthy thinking is going to properly heal every type of disease or injury.

So many such people seem unable to blend practicality with their theoretical beliefs. The result is that religious idiosyncrasies compound more tragedies and deaths. One such sect, with similar beliefs, calls itself the Peculiar People — at least they're practical when it comes to self-appraisal!

Religious 'cop-outs'

Some monks and nuns must incur the unfortunate description of being hypocritical, despite their dedication to a mainly laudable life-style. They start by 'officially' denying themselves the normality of a sexual life. This immediately throws them into conflict with *their* God, as they are denying his acknowledged (by them) purpose that man and woman are on this earth to reproduce the species — so why should they opt out of that? But what compounds their 'crime' is that, like it or not, they have the same, normal sexual desires as any other human which, just as normally, require an outlet.

It appears that quite a number 'like it' rather than 'not' from the numerous stories (too numerous and authenticated to dismiss all) that filter out, from time to time, about 'illicit' heterosexual affairs. That their desires sometimes also take the outlets of homosexuality and lesbianism, is another and unavoidable result of their supposed, but untenable sexual abstinence.

Monastic existence is also, in many ways, an easy 'cop-out' from life. By their chosen isolation, they remove themselves from the everyday temptations of life and therefore from the responsibility of having to face up to them, as the rest of us do. Far more admirable is the ordinary person who meets the challenge of daily living and succeeds by facing the problems rather than by sidestepping them.

"According to Jason Berry's astonishing, disheartening new account, *Lead Us Not into Temptation* (Doubleday), 400 U.S. and Canadian Catholic clerics have been accused of child molestation, costing the church roughly $400 million in damage payments and other expenses."

Time, December 14, 1992

" . . .costing the **church**", hardly . . . surely those paying the wages of sin for these heinous crimes are the church's members and congregations.

Quotations about Catholicism by Catholics . . .

"I cannot hide my indignation that some of the most illustrious Catholic cities are tainted with moral plague and loose ways to such a point that many monasteries designed to shelter virgins dedicated to God have now been turned into brothels. Can there be anything more abject and infamous?

Cardinal Gaspare Contarini

* * *

The index of forbidden books: " . . . the finest secret device ever invented for applying religion to the purpose of making men stupid".

Fra Paolo Sarpi

* * *

"The church is full of thieves, mercenaries and wolves."

Archbishop Marcel Lefebvre 1977

. . . and a personal opinion

The 'easiest' religions are those like Catholicism. It has rigid, documented sets of rules. They clearly lay down what is right and what is wrong – in their eyes. This is easy to follow, as it never necessitates moral decisions by the individual. He already 'knows' if it is right or not. Even if it's not, he can go ahead anyway, secure in the knowledge that he only has to go and confess – before going out to do it again. Confession is certainly cheaper that the psychiatrist's couch – if one doesn't count the cost of being confined in a personal mental prison

* * *

Is it remotely possible that anyone would consider conducting his business, based on an instruction manual written some 2,000 years ago and mis-translated countless times into a variety of languages? Pretty certainly not. However, it is quite remarkable how many millions of people conduct their lives according to just such an outdated manual . . . the bible.

Religious brainwashing

A number of religions, most widely exemplified by Catholicism, deliberately set out to deny and suppress the individual's freedom of choice in personal matters. Is this not an unjustified intrusion into the most fundamental of all privacies, the right to choose one's own way of life and code of behavior? We were not put on earth to be dictated to by any priesthood, and each individual's birthright should be the freedom to think and decide for himself.

Such religions seem unable, or unwilling, to recognize the difference between *offering* suggestions as to moral conduct and codes of religious and personal behavior . . . and *imposing* them on people, especially children — with terrifying threats of the consequences of failure to obey their strictures. Would it not be fairer to give all young people a religious education which recognizes and explains the simplified basics of the world's major religions? Later, when ready, they could make a choice, of their own free will, as to which, if any, they wished to follow.

Catholic logic?

Is not one of the ironies of the Catholic religion that a person can commit what is euphemistically known as a 'mistake' by killing a fellow human being — and be absolved for it in confession? Another person can make the 'mistake' of marrying someone with whom the relationship doesn't happen to work out. Instead of being pardoned for this *comparatively* harmless mistake, be allowed to divorce and start again — they are condemned by this religion to remain together in total misery. What an irony that an organization that will not permit its staff to marry, has so much to say about its members' marriages. On what grounds do they base their 'learned' rulings about such a highly complex subject? It certainly can't be personal experience . . .

"He that is without sin . . ."

The Anglican Church will not permit the remarriage of a divorcee in church under any circumstances. Are the *people* who make such harsh, uncompromising rulings such perfect, faultless, super-human beings who have never made a mistake in their lives? "He that is without sin among you, let *him* first cast a stone at her." (The woman taken in adultery.)

A 'modern crusader's' balance

Having criticized most of the major religions, what about the Protestants? It's hard to think of any *major* idiot syncrasy of theirs, apart from virgin birth — an interdenominational classic, which conveniently overlooks Joseph.

Back to square one

Obviously, religions are not all 'bad' and do some 'good'. Equally obviously, religions, like everything, contain many intermediate shades of gray between my black and white extremes. But I have intentionally highlighted the 'bad' sides, to shock people into thinking, *for themselves,* about aspects they may never have considered. So, having attacked most of the major religious beliefs, let me reiterate my opening remarks about the distilled essence of all religions: ". . . the existence of a power greater than man — unproven, but a mental need in most people. More practically: to aim to do a maximum of conscious good and a minimum of conscious evil in our allotted life span." An irrefutable summation of the *basic* beliefs of most of the major religions — and all that is *practically* needed to lead a worth while 'religious' life.

"There's only one problem with religions that have all the answers. They don't allow any questions."

Quote of unknown origin

8
ACTING . . . THE ILLUSION AND THE REALITY

This chapter is only included in deference to the understandable curiosity many people have about anything that goes on behind the scenes in the acting profession. Acting is the business of creating the illusion of reality and the ensuing passages will perhaps reveal some of the harsher realities less known to the public, who view a performance from 'out front', or read of the 'glamour world' in the glossy magazines.

Actors and actresses are subjected to a strangely paradox public assessment. Historically they have been regarded as 'wandering minstrels, rogues and vagabonds'. Yet, when they pass a certain, indefinable point in public esteem, they are virtually deified — a shattering transition from which a number of artists have never been known to recover!

Contrary to public belief, they are not all promiscuous ego-maniacs. The vast majority are dedicated professionals, who quietly ply their trade:- to bring pleasure to others.

Off-stage, they live as quiet, 'normal' lives as their frequently impoverished circumstances will permit. Many of them are painfully shy about appearing in public in any way other than on-stage, playing a role, for many only come out of themselves, when they can get into the words and part of the character they are portraying. Certainly there are a few headline seekers who crave that every moment of their lives receives publicity and whose best 'performances' are invariably given off-stage. They are epitomized by the starlets who can always be seen at movie premieres (and in prodoocers' beds), but never on the screen.

Actors and actresses

Many are forced to be poor, dedicated souls, obliged to live in a twilight zone of conditional promises and compromised reality, while little 'executive' ego-maniacs dangle 'carrots' in front of them and even pull the strings which make them jump for the carrots. Rejection can be a way of life for them.

Successful acting = living

To be a successful performer, an actor should always remember the valued old adage about looking at his fellow actors and listening to them. Apart from that, the best advice for any would-be, or existing actor who wants to learn how to create 'the illusion or reality' — is to learn everything he can about the actual reality of life. Some actors, particularly those who start in their early teens and even before, can be divorced from the reality of the world outside their fantasy half-world. Subsequently, their attempts to portray reality can fail to rise above the level of ridiculous, overdrawn caricatures.

Off-stage

In a strictly non-theatrical sense, it's far better to be an 'actor' (a doer), than a 'reactor' on the stage of life.

Films vs theatre

In acting, the stage had a very limited appeal for me. It hardly went beyond the opening night, for after that, apart from minor improvements, it became repetitious. Repetition, to me, is stagnation in life. Many actors profess to prefer it as the only 'true acting', where one gives a sustained performance. While not disputing this, I also feel there should be added as reasons: the traditional snobbery that stage acting is "the only real thing, dahling"; the fact that many actors crave and need the adulation of a live audience (the most extreme example I ever worked with, was a man who took his curtain calls, bowing — with his head *up* to watch the audience applauding him!), and lastly, because it provides the security of regular employment. The converse is the spectre that always haunts the actor.

Films offer not only the challenge of doing something different every day — you do a passage, perfect it and immortalize it — but you can later learn from watching your performance how to improve it — an impossibility with theatre work. Films also offer the opportunity to travel and so to learn about other people and their cultures. Also, each role enables you to learn about another profession. You may also have to operate equipment and mix with real workers or professionals in their own milieu.

A further point: the actor's function — as an integral part of a production which should be doing the same thing — is 'to create the illusion of reality' for the audience. In a film this is totally possible. Not only is much of what the viewer sees absolutely real, but the remainder is indistinguishable from reality — so completing the illusion.

In the theatre, the actors are up there in front of you — within touching distance. They are limited by the proscenium arch, walls and doors which tremble, the obviously false props and reconstructions of exterior locations. Their limitations at achieving credibility are legion. Lastly, at the end of the performance, they all step out of character and take their bows as *themselves* — including the resurrected dead bodies. The illusion is completely shattered. When you leave a film, the illusion remains intact.

The stage is a great place for musicals, opera, ballet and even experimental theatre — spheres of activity which never take place in real life. But I feel straight drama has no place in the theatre. It is attempting to imitate reality and that should be left to the realm of films and TV. They are so much better equipped to handle it.

"There's no sickness like show sickness . . ."

What kind of a man offers a girl (or a boy) a part in a film or TV show, in return for going to bed with him? A man who doesn't think enough of himself, to have a girl go to bed with him for what he is as a man. This poor excuse for a man, can have no self-respect and virtually nothing to offer as a human being. It makes me wonder whatever qualified him to be in a position to offer the girl the doubtful value of the 'deal'. Between her 'sacrifice' and his shortcomings, they make a pretty sorry pair.

PR — and 'private relations'

Some artists spend huge sums of money on every conceivable aspect of public relations, to ensure that they become household names. Once having succeeded, many of them then spend even greater sums on what might be termed 'private relations', in an attempt to regain the privacy of life they have so successfully lost.

Real recognition

Many Showbiz personalities suffer great insecurities because they fear they are loved privately, or adulated publicly, *only* for their glamorized image and not for their real selves. Not that all of them are too sure where one leaves off and the other starts.

Real achievement

There's another problem facing some actors who have "made it" — whatever "it" is. They may still feel the need to find something *real* to achieve *solely by themselves*. It's all part of proving oneself.

Relative artistic activity

An actor is always waiting for someone else to give him work — a hideously frustrating position to be in. A singer can sing, a dancer can dance, a writer can write, a musician can play, a composer can compose and an artist can paint, draw or sculpt. Alone among the creative professions, the actor is unable to perform his art by himself. Mirrors, even wives and sweethearts may make fine, uncritical audiences, but something's still missing and besides, there are only so many soliloquies!

Relative artistic immortality

A writer's books and a singer's records etc., stay in the home and can pass from generation to generation. An actor's work doesn't stay in the home and generally lives a shorter public life than the writer's or singer's creations.

How to be an overnight success — in 17 years

Most actors are happy to be judged by the viewing public (or by their professional peers) and accepted or rejected by them. The reaction to a performer is pure and simple: audiences like or they don't like. The stumbling block most actors and actresses encounter in presenting themselves to the public, is the little men who sit nervously behind 'Hollywood' desks. They like to think they're doing the difficult job of assessing public taste. In reality, many are only victims of their own insecurities and frustrations (several were unsuccessful actors) and the fact that their position is often the only way they can "get themselves laid" — to use their own crude terminology.

Paranoiacally, they tend to regard 'male' actors as potential threats to their doubtful virility, and actresses as a means of bolstering it up. Often, if they are not catering to their own hang-ups, they are pandering to those of the person they work for — procuring, is the word used in other walks of life. Another paranoiac characteristic is the fear of making decisions that *might* commit them to the *possibility* of failure. Sheep-like, they prefer to ride the coat-tails of the few gutsy 'visionaries'. *They* are men who were prepared to back their own judgement and give newcomers and relatively unknown talent a chance to prove what they could do.

These 'visionaries' form part of the other side of the

Showbiz coin: a small, elite band of 'normal' executives, producers, directors, casting directors and agents who are genuinely dedicated to entertaining and informing the public — without always having to resort to pornography. They are people who understand the strange blend of commercial fact and artistic creativity. They also possess the alchemy required to transmute these two incompatible ingredients into *quality* box office gold. Among other attributes, is their ability to understand the half-world of the actor (many of them are also ex-actors) and treat him as a human being with feelings. To them he is not just a troublesome commodity, necessary to their search for a rainbow crock of 'instant wealth'.

Another difficulty of the actor's career, is not just the irregularity of employment, but the irregularity of progress and advancement. In most other careers, these factors are at least steady, but with the probability of advancement commensurate with exceptional talent and /or effort invested. Sometimes, an actor 'shoots to stardom overnight', but this is far rarer than the public are led to believe. The public love the 'Cinderella' overnight concept. It allows an identification with the possibility of it happening to 'the man in the street' — themselves. More realistic are the heartaches that lie behind the title of a famous singer's autobiography. *"How To Be An Overnight Success – In 17 Years!"*.

No one *has* to become an actor. It's a free choice, but a gamble. A gamble it most surely is, for far too often, the factor least considered is the performer's talent. It is pertinent to analogize that while a gambler at the tables risks only his money, a *talented* actor may gamble away his whole life to achieve recognition and a release from the years of privation, when it is almost too late — or, even, never at all. .. In the long process, he will have to watch many lesser talents, perhaps more prepared to compromise themselves, taking his place.

R.I.P. — A. N. Actor

I am often asked why I left the 'exciting, glamorous world of acting'. Whatever my particular ego is, it prefers to be itself, rather than play make-believe roles. So, my work in TV as a program producer /presenter, host, interviewer, quiz master, newscaster and continuity announcer is right for me. Also in my work as a journalist I have, whenever possible, fully participated in whatever assignment I was reporting on, rather than merely observing it. I have led a very active and involved *real* life and, even while acting, always maintained business and creative interests, as well as voluntary committee work.

My comments about acting should in no way be misconstrued as any censure of the acting profession. I regard it as an essential ingredient of life, especially in today's sombre world. I have nothing but the greatest respect and admiration for anyone who dedicates his or her life to providing people with enjoyment, and also stimulating their minds, through the medium of the entertainment business.

However, I recall hearing Tony Bennett being interviewed on radio about a film he was starring in; he described acting as being: " . . .beyond boredom." I can relate to his comment, from the following experience: I once did a commercial for London's Metropolitan Police Force, playing a surgeon. In three scenes, I put on a pair of surgical gloves, looked up at a clock and bent over an operating table. Time on screen . . . perhaps 6 seconds. Time to shoot them . . . 10 hours! The rest of the time was spent hanging around. In those ten hours, I could have recorded five or six half-hour interview programs, exercised my mind and felt I had achieved something worthwhile that day. As the 'surgeon', I didn't need a single grey cell to operate and to me, my day's 'achievement' was about as minimal as possible. Show Biz is definitely not all glamour, there *is* a lot of boredom and wasted time.

9
FROM DIARY TO BOOK

This little book was born, fittingly, in the world's philosophical heart – the Left Bank of Paris. In 1956, I sat in the tiny Club L'Abbaye, listening to the owners' soulful folk songs. Pensively, I stared at the candles . . . then whispered, to the delectable distraction coiled around me, the first words of a long-distant book: "Man clings to life as a flame clings to a wick when threatened by the wind, for the spark of life is so easily extinguished". Her expressive French body was more responsive to clinging than to philosophy and as I had no wish to be extinguished, she had little difficulty in persuading me to reciprocate!

Over the years, many more thoughts were scribbled down in diaries . . . when I managed to surface from similar distractions, for "clinging" continued to prove a major source of philosophical inspiration. Even Omar Khayyám and Goethe did some of their best work in the same circumstances!

**Why the book? Curiosity . . . it made me what I am today
. . . and will shape all my tomorrows.**

While reading, you may have wondered why I sometimes
write with sarcastic vehemence and at others, with
gentleness. If my writing were only the former, I could be
dismissed as just another 'angry young man', rebelling
against the established order of things in his generation.
Yes, I am angry, desperately, sadly angry — to look around
and see: a world filled with hate, misunderstanding and
greed which result in the atrocities of wars, torture, killings
and 'minor' assaults; men who will brainwash others, who
will lie, cheat and deceive in the pursuit of money, power
and women; religions which deliberately set out to possess
and control children's minds before they are old enough to
think and decide for themselves; religions which 'solicit'
contributions from poor people to make themselves ever
wealthier. I will always attack (with words — I abhor
violence) and expose to the harsh light of honesty anything
which I feel is cruel, unjust, corrupt, dishonest, fraudulent or
just humbug.

These are the evil sides of this world, which I dislike with a
passionate, burning intensity. But, with equal intensity, I
love and want to foster and publicize that which is good. I
admit to being a somewhat black-and-white character. I'm
positive and self-opinionated — but always prepared to
listen and learn, *or re-learn*. I don't claim that my opinions
are right — except for me — and for those who happen to
share my views. That is the lot of any critic; he is read by
those who *generally* agree with *most* of his opinions.

The evil and catastrophic aspects of life are continuously
forced into our minds by most news media: TV, radio,
newspapers and magazines. Unfortunately, most of them
believe that these sensational events make the headlines
which sell most newspapers, etc. Making money is what
most are primarily in business for. A few distinguished
exceptions believe their *first* duty is to inform the public.
Being subjected to a constant barrage of melodramatic
'news', is bound to condition us into accepting that it
represents the majority of life and human behavior. It just
isn't so.

One great pioneer believed in the value of 'good' and also proved it could be financially successful. Walt Disney's axiom and 'magic formula' was " . . . making good human stories where you can reach people and which prove that *the better things of life can be as interesting as the sordid things."* (my italics). The huge financial empire he left behind is witness to the correctness of his beliefs. However, he always successfully blended 'horror' into his films, but as a balanced ingredient of life, *not its totality.*

Some of my opinions may have seemed caustic, even cruel — especially in some generalizations. They are *only* generalizations, have only the value of any generalization and are subject to all their many exceptions. However, they are opinions honestly expressed as observations of what I saw. I don't know of any axe I have to grind deliberately, except that of honesty. I am not aware of any other conscious biases — but allow there can always be unconscious ones. I don't gush theatrically over everything and say: "It's all simply wonderful, dahling." Like or dislike, it's all expressed from my heart.

Since as far back as I can remember, I questioned everything that passed before me and never knowingly accepted anything blindly — especially the absurd dictums handed down through the ages by the anonymous body of *theys:* the *theys* who say this is done or isn't done, is good taste or bad taste. I recall challenging my parents on what they said was 'accepted' good taste, in, for instance, music and art. I simply and logically claimed that if you presented 12 people with a piece of music or a painting, you would most likely get 12 different opinions, ranging from total adoration to total rejection — and varying shades of gray in between.

I subject everything to the acid test of logic and common sense and only accept or reject in the light of their findings. Most of us are brought up and conditioned to accept unquestioningly the dictums of parents and teachers. Then we find, years later, when it's generally too late to change already formed behavior patterns, that many of the dictums don't make much sense.

I never try to *force* anyone to think or believe as I do and I can't abide the missionary who threatens hellfire for those who reject him. I will only lay out, for others to sample, whatever facts or opinions have made sense and a better life for me. If they find them palatable, well and good. If they turn out to be indigestible, that's fine too. Each person must find himself, in his own way, not by being forced into it, but by being *offered* guidance to take or reject, as he thinks fit.

Undoubtedly I will have angered some people, by attacking their beliefs. I can only hope they are very honest with themselves and are certain that their 'righteous' anger is not a cover-up for not wanting to face the truth my comments may have exposed. It's not easy to look at oneself with brutal honesty and it can be very disturbing to have to do so after creating and believing in a 'front', carefully built up over many years.

Some of those 'disturbed' can build a better and more honest life, even though my challenge may seem to have torn down the whole foundation of their lives. If that was the case, it means they recognized their foundations were 'feet of clay' and not 'the solid rock'.

It's supposed to take courage or stupidity to be frank enough to say what you feel and 'damn the consequences' — which implies that you couldn't care less. I don't damn them. I care very much. Otherwise, I wouldn't have put myself through a number of experiences, many of them not too pleasant, to further understand and have more compassion for others. Nor would I have written this book.

I used to be very intolerant as a child and although traces will be still noticeable in some of my comments (!), I express my beliefs very frankly, in the hope that they will make some people's lives happier and fuller. Life must be based on the firm rock of self-honesty, not on the quicksand of self-delusion. I've tried that, too — what a waste of time! No, I do not damn the consequences — I hope for them.

Whatever passes before me in life moves me to react. Although I *feel* happiness and sadness with equal intensity, the *reaction* cannot be the same. Something 'good' — which can be no more than the observation of a moment of man or nature — need only be recorded to share the happiness. Something 'evil': cruel, unjust, false or stupid, provokes an intense desire to expose the problem to everyone who might do something to rectify it — if only they knew of its existence, or its effect on them. That 'good' and 'evil' tumble over each other in bewildering confusion, is an accurate and eloquent reflection of the journey of life, which has its highlights — and balancing lowlights: the patchwork quilt of all life.

One important lesson I learned from extensive travel — which I needed to learn — was tolerance. What is 'right', 'acceptable' and 'normal' in one part of the world, will quite certainly be 'wrong', 'unacceptable' and 'abnormal' somewhere else. If we can accept, and therefore tolerate, this difference of customs on an international scale, it's not too hard to bring it down to the level of day-to-day, personal living. That I may disagree with your opinion, doesn't necessarily mean that you're wrong. You're 'right' for you and I'm 'right' for me. Hopefully, peaceful co-existence starts at this man-to-man level and someday may percolate up to embrace all men.

You may wonder why I presumed to set down ideas on life and living while I was only in my mid-thirties. In my few years, I have lived an unusually full life. Most of it has been positively and constructively orientated, but it also contained more than enough of the negative, down sides of life. I started traveling on my own aged 13, have since circled the globe and been in some 75 countries. Speaking and writing French, German, Italian and Spanish, having had many jobs and playing most team and individual sports, enabled me to sample the work and play of many people — some more deeply than others, naturally. So I learned something of living and others' lives, by exposing myself to many facets of life. Sometimes it was a bit 'rough', but that was the only way I could gain the experience I wanted — and needed to write this book.

Hopefully, it will have helped others to realize they are not as alone as they think, in their hopes and aims, *and* in the problems and fears encountered in the quest to achieve them. That some passages may have appeared as trite old truisms, dressed up in new clothes, in no way invalidates them. The new clothing may have appealed to the comprehension of some who had previously missed their meaning and anyway, none of us knows all of them in any form!

**The cover of the book in its original form.
(Drawn by Maz from a design by the author.)**

Publishing

The following passage appeared in *Philosov Cocktail,* the original 1970 publication of this book, under the heading 'Publishing one's own book':

I took the unusual (but not unprecedented) step of publishing this book myself, mainly because – at this point in my life – the manuscript was unlikely to be regarded by most publishers as a 'sure-fire commercial *success'. The nature of today's business world decrees that there are, regrettably, but understandably, fewer people who can afford to publish a creative work – which could be of value to people – without being virtually assured of a fair financial return. If I had been a well-known figure in any sphere of public life, my words and thoughts would have been saleable from the name-value of the 'personality'. For the 'unknowns', there are few of yesterday's patrons of the arts.*

I therefore decided I was neither prepared to wait till achieving 'personality' status, nor was I prepared to gamble on finding the publisher who would recognize, not only the import of its contents, but also the long-term commercial potential of the book. Years could be wasted in such a search, as respective publishers took 3-5 months rejecting, what they might have considered was a manuscript which did not equate with instant cash return. Kahil Gibran's beautiful book, The Prophet, *was (in common with innumerable meritorious works in every area of artistic endeavor) rejected by many publishers, before becoming one of the world's most treasured books. World famous books which were first published privately by their authors include:* Robinson Crusoe, Ulysses, Betty Zane *and the* Rubáiyát of Omar Khayyám.

What finally decided me to publish it myself, was my belief in its purpose: to help people face and resolve the problems of daily living and of their whole lives. This is the first step towards creating inner peace within an individual, which – in turn – is the first move towards achieving international peace, through understanding and tolerance, between all men. A man cannot be expected to live in peace with his fellow-men, if he cannot live in peace with himself.

Back to the beginning and into the future

Thank you for joining me thus far on my journey through life. I sincerely hope the book has added something to your understanding of yourself, other people and of life itself — and so given you a new dimension of happiness and contentment for all your days.

The book started with the words of *Prayer For Peace* by Saint Francis of Assisi, to whom it owes much of its existence. It therefore seems appropriate to close with a summation of my philosophy of life, conveyed in his style of wording:

May I not so much seek to be informed, as to inform;
To learn, as to teach;
For it is by informing and teaching that we learn most.

Let me not so much want to be entertained, as to entertain;
To be made happy, as to give happiness;
For it is by entertaining and giving, that we achieve happiness.

. . . AND AFTER THE BOOK

After writing, compiling and publishing this book, I came across a well-known passage, written in 1692 and found in Old Saint Paul's Church in Baltimore, the home of the American half of my family.

The few, simple words which follow, express most of what I've taken a whole book to say . . . thus making it largely superfluous!

DESIDERATA

GO PLACIDLY AMID THE NOISE & HASTE, & REMEMBER WHAT PEACE THERE MAY BE IN SILENCE. AS FAR AS POSSIBLE WITHOUT surrender be on good terms with all persons. Speak your truth quietly & clearly; and listen to others, even the dull & ignorant; they too have their story. ﹏ Avoid loud & aggressive persons, they are vexations to the spirit. If you compare yourself with others, you may become vain & bitter; for always there will be greater & lesser persons than yourself. Enjoy your achievements as well as your plans. ﹏ Keep interested in your own career, however humble; it is a real possession in the changing fortunes of time. Exercise caution in your business affairs; for the world is full of trickery. But let this not blind you to what virtue there is; many persons strive for high ideals; and everywhere life is full of heroism. ﹏ Be yourself. Especially, do not feign affection. Neither be cynical about love; for in the face of all aridity & disenchantment it is perennial as the grass. ﹏ Take kindly the counsel of the years, gracefully surrendering the things of youth. Nurture strength of spirit to shield you in sudden misfortune. But do not distress yourself with imaginings. Many fears are born of fatigue & loneliness. Beyond a wholesome discipline, be gentle with yourself. ﹏ You are a child of the universe, no less than the trees & the stars; you have a right to be here. And whether or not it is clear to you, no doubt the universe is un-folding as it should. ﹏ Therefore be at peace with God, whatever you conceive Him to be, and whatever your labors & aspirations, in the noisy confusion of life keep peace with your soul. ﹏ With all its sham, drudgery & broken dreams, it is still a beautiful world. Be careful. Strive to be happy. ﹏ ﹏

A closing thought

LIVE AS YOU WILL
HAVE WISHED TO
HAVE LIVED WHEN
YOU ARE DYING.

GELLERT
b. July 4, 1715

INDEX

2 LIVING WITH ONESELF   47

8 ACTING . . . THE ILLUSION AND THE REALITY   173

9 FROM DIARY TO BOOK   181

. . . AND AFTER THE BOOK   189